D1592612

THE WORLD CRISIS BY WINSTON CHURCHILL
A CRITICISM

THE WORLD CRISIS
by WINSTON CHURCHILL

A CRITICISM

by

COLONEL THE LORD SYDENHAM OF COMBE

ADMIRAL SIR REGINALD BACON

GENERAL SIR FREDERICK MAURICE

GENERAL SIR W. D. BIRD

SIR CHARLES OMAN

WITH MAPS AND CHARTS

KENNIKAT PRESS
Port Washington, N. Y./London

THE WORLD CRISIS BY WINSTON CHURCHILL: A CRITICISM

First published in 1928
Reissued in 1970 by Kennikat Press
Library of Congress Catalog Card No: 71-105856
ISBN 0-8046-1041-X

Manufactured by Taylor Publishing Company   Dallas, Texas

PREFACE

PARTS I and II of the third volume of *The World Crisis* deals with many important issues that arose during the Great War. When writing those pages Mr. Winston Churchill could hardly claim to possess expert knowledge on several of the subjects with which he has dealt. The result has been that many of the conclusions he has formed are inaccurate and the theories he has formulated unsound.

Throughout these volumes runs the refrain: " If I, Winston Churchill, had been listened to ; if I had had the direction of affairs, then thousands of lives would have been saved and the war shortened by many months."

One of the main lines of argument advanced in support of this assumption is set forth at length in the chapter in *The World Crisis* entitled " The Blood Test." In this chapter Mr. Churchill has marshalled figures and, as an amateur in so intricate a subject as war losses, expounded the meaning they conveyed to him. In the chapter in the present book, " The Losses on the Somme," Sir Charles Oman, who, from his occupation during the war, has a very detailed knowledge of the German losses, disputes Mr. Churchill's arguments and clearly shows that the true figures, intelligently handled, completely upset his theories and vitiate his conclusions. His views on the military strategy of the war suffer further severe handling in two other chapters, one by Major-

General Sir F. Maurice, and the other by Major-General Sir W. Bird.

He is no happier when dealing with Jutland. Here errors in his facts mar his description of the fight, and his suggestions of what should have been done at the critical points of the battle show a superficiality of sea knowledge which is astonishing in one who has occupied the post of First Lord of the Admiralty.

The very attractiveness of Mr. Churchill's writing of itself constitutes a danger; for the layman may well be led to accept facile phrase and seductive argument for hard fact and sober reasoning.

The above considerations have led to the publication of the present volume. It is not a comprehensive criticism of *The World Crisis*, Volume III, but is merely a collection of criticisms written by experts each responsible only for his own contributions, but each having particular knowledge of the subject with which he deals. These go far to destroy any claim Volume III of *The World Crisis* may have to historical value.

The chapter entitled 'Mr. Churchill as Historian' is reprinted from the *Quarterly Review*. That of 'The German Losses on the Somme' from the *Nineteenth Century and After*. That of 'Mr. Churchill's Opinions : Some other Points of View' from the *Army Quarterly*; and portions of the chapter 'Joffre, Galliéni and the Marne' have appeared in the *Contemporary Review*.

The thanks of the authors are due to the editors of these journals for their kind permission to reprint.

CONTENTS

CHAPTER I

MR. CHURCHILL AS HISTORIAN
By LORD SYDENHAM OF COMBE

THE story of war has fascinated mankind in all ages. The characteristics and the fate of great nations can be traced in pages which record shining deeds of heroism and self-sacrifice, brilliant examples of devoted patriotism, masterpieces of naval and military achievement, and failures pregnant with warning. The glamour which once illumined the battlefield on sea and land seems to have faded. Science has provided death-dealing weapons operating with mass effect in forms which appal the imagination. At the same time detailed descriptions, vivid and terrifying, are now widely disseminated, tending to cause war in general to be regarded as the worst of human evils, unnecessary and to be avoided at any cost. We know only in rough outline what happened at Salamis. The tragedy of the battle cruisers at Jutland has been painted in words that all can understand, and photographs now enable us to visualise disaster. The prolonged horrors which accompanied the retreat of the Grand Army from Moscow in 1812 are in great part shrouded from our eyes ; but the sufferings of our magnificent troops in the paralysing mud of the trenches in Flanders and in Gallipoli and Mesopotamia have been brought home to us, and will haunt the memory of at least one generation. Internationalism being now in fashion, and

Socialism being held up as the ideal which mankind must strive to attain, it is well to remember that Socialist theories, applied on the grand scale in Russia, have already caused a greater loss of human life, with suffering in more cruel forms, than the Great War.

How should history, including the history of war which, so far as we can see, mankind can never relegate to Saturn, be written? There is no agreement among the pandits; but a strain of fiction seems to be accepted as desirable. One authority has recently announced that, 'Even if truth has its uses, history is not the place for it.' Truth, however, still has 'its uses,' which democracies ignore, and if the past is to afford any teaching, it must find some 'place' in history. Mr. Baldwin has shrewdly suggested that a certain measure of personal bias is necessary to make history tolerable to the general reader; but it is not easy to adjust the personal equation. Carlyle and Macaulay, in whose works bias was rampant, are eminently readable, and to the Duke of Wellington the latter appeared to be a master of his craft. Both have—irretrievably in many minds—injured the cause of truth.

The Great War stands out above all others in the intense complexity and novelty of its world-ranging operations, and in its revelation of the noblest qualities of the British peoples at the zenith of their capacity for united action and shared sacrifice. It is replete with records of gallantry never surpassed in our annals, and, as never before, to be lavishly found not only in the ranks of a professional navy and army, but among all classes of a whole nation in arms. It abounds with lessons of all kinds, going deeper than strategy and tactics to the political foundations of the State. All this and more must be faithfully registered lest we forget, even though half a century may be needed before the involved series of tremendous events can be placed in true perspective.

Mr. Churchill's two final volumes complete a work in which the interest never flags. As a descriptive writer, he has few if any equals, and he paints alike men and happenings in vivid phrases which cling to the memory. His rhetoric is often dazzling ; but here and there it strays dangerously near to the line at which bathos supervenes. There is bias in plenty, which leads to judgments challenging criticism, while a far-ranging imagination induces speculations into the might-have-beens which, in war as in politics, may be barren of profit as well as misleading. In the first of these volumes Mr. Churchill goes back to the beginning of the war by recalling the wonderfully accurate forecast of General Michel in 1911 and his inspired plan of campaign, which were ruthlessly rejected by French military opinion. The von Schlieffen plan had come to maturity before this time and was being perfected in detail by the Germans ; but the French ' General Staff did not believe that Germany would make a turning movement through Belgium, certainly not through Northern Belgium,' and the ' offensive school,' led by Colonel Grandmaison, settled down to Plan XVII, which proved totally unsuited to the conditions in August 1914, and has since been riddled by French criticism. General Michel fell, and the execution of this disastrous plan rested with General Joffre, whose capacity Mr. Churchill somewhat underrates, because he ' had never commanded an army nor directed ground manœuvres even in a War Game,' though he possessed qualities which ' fitted him to render most useful service to the various fleeting French administrations which preceded the conflict.'

Thus, at the start, political considerations deflected the course of the terrific ' Battle of the Frontiers,' and, as the older von Moltke laid down, mistakes in the first dispositions of the troops cannot be remedied. In spite of what Mr. Churchill calls ' almost fatal errors ' on our side, the Schlieffen plan miscarried, and Paris was saved, partly by the timely retreat of General Lanrezac and Sir John French and partly by the dramatic intervention of General Galliéni, but also by certain mistakes of the German General Staff. The immediate and critical situation was relieved ; but the French lost nearly 330,000 men, including a great part of the flower of their regular army, expended in most gallant attacks, badly directed though heroically led, against overwhelming numbers. The victory of the Marne, followed by the German retreat, blinded us to some important facts by which the whole course of the war was prejudiced, and Mr. Churchill rightly states that ' the magnitude and terror ' of the tremendous Battle of the Frontiers ' is scarcely now known to British consciousness.'

That France remained undaunted and ready for vast new efforts is a striking proof of the fortitude of her people. The chapter entitled ' The Blood Test,' in which the author surveys the war on the Western Front from the point of view of the huge casualty lists, is painful reading. The prolonged agony of the combatant nations is here set down in cold figures, the full import of which we happily did not realise at the time. These grisly statistics are handled with much skill, but they are open to serious criticism, because the returns on which they are based are not strictly comparable ; while the varying circumstances in which they occurred vitiate conclusions drawn from lumped totals.[1] Major-General Sir F. Maurice, attacking Mr. Churchill's deductions, has stated that he has,

' by omitting lightly wounded, under-estimated the total German casualties on the Western Front by approximately 1,300,000. . . . I am certain that he has greatly exaggerated the British battle casualties.'[2]

Sir Charles Oman, M.P., has powerfully reinforced these conclusions,[3] and the danger of attempting to base theories upon statistics is manifest. Mr. Churchill discredits the whole strategic conception of the Westerners, finds fault with the views of Sir Douglas Haig, and especially

[1] The overwhelming superiority of the German artillery in the earlier stages of the war, and our culpable deficiency in machine-guns, the use of which had been carefully studied in Berlin, are factors which Mr. Churchill does not adequately regard.
[2] *The Times*, March 17.
[3] *Nineteenth Century and After*, May 1927.

those of Sir William Robertson, and suggests that other methods and different strategic policies would have hastened the end and saved life on a large scale. Attacks on well-conceived defences created in the field have always been costly, and on the Western Front the Germans lavished the art of the military engineer to an extent never approached in the past. To attack such intensely formidable lines as quickly grew up in front of the Allies required tactical experience, which could be gained only by fighting and then gradually, an overpowering artillery, which for many months existed only on the German side, and the Tank, slowly evolved and at first misused. In part at least, all that Mr. Churchill sweepingly condemns in the policy of the Westerners must be attributed to the total and inevitable inadequacy of our preparations at the outbreak of war, to the continuous and insistent need for supporting with insufficient means, the measures to which the French were committed, and to the blighting influence of Plan XVII.

Mistakes were freely made on the Western Front, as in the misconceived and therefore futile attack on the Dardanelles, or the mad advance with a tired and ill-equipped force on Bagdad. All this must be admitted ; but the crash finally came in the West and was due to the heavy losses, to the wearing down of the German *moral*, and to the exhaustion of man-power arising from the offensives of the Allies. Mr. Churchill underestimates at 3,348,000 the total German losses on the Western Front before Ludendorff's great attack beginning in March 1918; but he explains the drain on German man-power, the annual intake of which had to be ' heavily anticipated . . . in their hard need.' Yet he is convinced that ' It was their own offensive, not ours, that consummated their ruin. They were worn down not by Joffre, Nivelle, and Haig, but by Ludendorff.' But for what had been learned in the terrific fighting that preceded, with the shaking of the German *moral* which it entailed, Ludendorff's tremendous effort might have succeeded. But for the failure to reinforce the British armies in time, it might have taken other forms. Throughout these volumes there is a stream of suggestion that there are ways of avoiding costly offensives, by indirect methods pursuing lines of least resistance, which to politicians watching the long, bloody, and apparently abortive operations in the West seemed naturally attractive.

Mr. Lloyd George had a great inspiration which appeared on January 1, 1915. He proposed to withdraw our Expeditionary Force with the exception of a reserve to be retained near Boulogne and to send it to the Balkans to operate in vague conjunction with the armies of Serbia, Greece, and Rumania against Austria. At the same time 100,000 British troops were to be landed somewhere in Syria to cut off the Turks, believed to be moving on Egypt. The effect of this wild-cat scheme would have been the conquest of France, the loss of the Channel ports, and a German triumph. Mr. Churchill, though a ' whole hogger ' as regards the Dardanelles, does not appear to be a too enthusiastic Easterner, and he sharply condemns the original occupation of the pestilential area of Salonica.

'Such was their (M. Briand's and Mr. Lloyd George's) influence upon events that a numerous allied army was, at enormous cost, in defiance of military opinion, and after most of the original political objectives had disappeared, carried or being carried to Salonica.'

Later, this army was to make good after unnecessary loss and wasteful expenditure. While, however, Mr. Churchill is thus quick to note the gross defects of Mr. Lloyd George's first contribution to war strategy, he asks us to ' Suppose, for instance, the war power represented by the 450,000 French and British casualties in the Champagne-Loos battle of 1915 had been used to force the Dardanelles and combine the Balkan States '!

Such profitless imaginings could be multiplied —and parodied—indefinitely. In all, we employed nearly 470,000 troops at Gallipoli and lost about 120,000 killed and wounded, exclusive of heavy casualties from sickness, while 74,000 tons of war shipping were sunk, and the drain upon our resources was very great. The Expedition was happily withdrawn after risky delays caused by vacillations in council. The whole tragic story has been vividly told by Sir W. Robertson,[1] who is able to supplement the Report of the Royal

[1] *Soldiers and Statesmen* (Cassell and Co.).

Commission, and it is unjust to attribute this lamentable fiasco ' to the narrow and local views of British Admirals and Generals and of the French Headquarters.' Mr. Churchill considers that, even in 1916, a ' surprise attack upon the Dardanelles . . . would best have served our interests.' But ' no such audacious scheme crossed the minds of our rulers,' and

> ' It was not until the summer of 1918 that Admiral Keyes—strong in the achievement of Zeebrugge—and Admiral Wemyss, installed as First Sea Lord, were able to obtain the authority for a renewed naval forcing of the Dardanelles in the possible campaign of 1919. That was at last too late.'

It was indeed ' too late,' since all the conditions which justified the original project had passed away long before this ' authority ' was forthcoming.

In didactic mood, Mr. Churchill outlines his policy as regards the handling of the whole campaign in France and Flanders, and the tactical conceptions which he sketches with a light hand, colour much of his abundant military criticism. His policy is defined as an ' active defensive.' ' Suppose,' he writes, ' that we,

> ' both British and French, have trained our armies behind the trench line to a high standard of flexible manœuvring efficiency ; suppose we have permanently fortified, with concrete and every modern device, those portions of the front where we cannot retreat ; suppose we have long

selected and shrewdly weakened those portions where we could afford to give 20 or 30 kilometres of ground ; suppose that we lure the enemy to attack them and make great pockets and bulges in a thin and yielding front, and then, just as he thinks himself pressing on to final victory, strike with independent counter-offensive on the largest scale and with deeply planned railways, not at his fortified trench line, but at the flanks of a moving, quivering line of battle ' !

To this general policy artifice should have been added.

' Craft, forcsight, deep comprehension of the verities, not only local but general ; stratagems, devices, manœuvres, all of these on the grand scale are demanded from the chiefs of great armies.'

These are manifestly counsels of perfection based upon experiences dearly bought ; but it is un- likely that they entirely escaped the purview of the generals whom Mr. Churchill criticises. It must be admitted that our splendid infantry was sometimes used before it was fully trained to ' a high standard of flexible manœuvring efficiency ' ; but valiant attempts were made to ' make great pockets and bulges,' and their comparative failure was in great part due to conditions which Mr. Churchill ignores. The enemy's ' fortified trench line ' had in any case to be broken through on a broad front before the ' quivering ' flanks of his army could be attacked, and when this had been accomplished much time was required to bring the artillery to new positions and to organise supply. Such efforts, and notably that of Ludendorff in 1918, always came to a standstill during which the threatened forces could draw upon reserves and create a new defensive line. Mr. Churchill's policy would have been to ' lure the enemy ' to make these ' bulges ' just where it suited our preparations ; but the Germans, though committing gigantic errors in his opinion, were well served in the matter of information, and in vain is the snare if the bird has observed it. Our armies were never free to adopt an independent policy, but were forced to conform to conditions either arising in France or prescribed by the enemy. The fighting of 1916 was dominated by Falkenhayn's decision to make a mass attack on Verdun, which Mr. Churchill regards as dictated by a hopelessly false strategy. That of 1917 was virtually ordained by the ' Nivelle experiment,' deranged from the first by Ludendorff's sudden withdrawal. In that of 1918, German initiative governed the action of the Allied generals until the general advance to victory.

In the form of a ' Political Interlude ' (Chapter X) Mr. Churchill deals with some of the political reactions which powerfully affected the course of the war. Of the break-up of the Asquith Cabinet and its implications, he has much to tell. In July 1915 he drew up an important report for the Cabinet, the gist of which was that the then methods of recruiting were unjust and inadequate. The time for ordered conscription had come, though this was not stated, and divisions in the Cabinet made a ' thorough discussion ' impossibly dangerous. The personal differences of leading politicians thus prevented the truth from being laid before Parliament and the nation. ' Many weeks slipped away in deadlock,' and at length the Derby scheme was evolved as a compromise, well intentioned and well directed, but quite insufficient to meet the realities of the military situation. Further prolonged political complications followed, and after consideration by numerous committees the new Man Power Bill was not introduced in the House of Commons till April 9, 1917, and was quickly passed though not wholly satisfactory. Over these protracted proceedings Mr. Churchill skates too lightly; but happily Sir W. Robertson has filled up the gaps and explained the great efforts of the soldiers to bring home the dire needs of the situation to successive Cabinets.

With the setting up of the Lloyd George Government in December 1916 a new political era dawned, and new vigour was imparted, in certain respects, to the tremendous national effort; but fresh strategic inspiration was not apparent. Mr. Churchill claims the fortunate destruction of ' a series of absurd conventions.'

' The first and most monstrous of these was that the Generals and Admirals were more competent to deal with the broad issues of the war than abler men in other spheres of life.'

Much might be written about this ' most mon-

strous ' convention, and it is admitted that the
' abler men ' should prevail in council; but the
underlying assumption that ' national leaders,'
upon whom democracy has thoughtlessly conferred
position in peace time, are able to dispense with
long study of war and to become instantly fit to
' stand by Cæsar and give directions,' needs
qualification. Any attempt to estimate the
respective contributions of these ' national
leaders ' and of the professional chiefs to the
changing scenes in the great world tragedy could
only lead to interminable controversy. Both—
French and British—played essential parts.
Neither could perform the rôle falling to the
other.

Mr. Churchill pays a well-deserved tribute to
the qualities of Mr. Lloyd George ; but, in view
of his many admonitions and of his speech at the
secret session of Parliament, he ' cannot acquit the
Prime Minister of his responsibility ' for not
stopping the ' offensive in France.' He even
makes it clear that Mr. Lloyd George's curious
fascination by Nivelle led to proceedings which
the military chiefs regarded with grave misgivings.
He is entitled to claim credit for the First Minister
of the Crown, who at least sanctioned ' the convoy
system, which broke the U-boat attack at sea ; the
forward impulsion in Palestine which overwhelmed
the Turks, and the unified command which in-
augurated the crowning victory in France.' But
if Mr. Lloyd George was really working for a
Generalissimo, he moved by ' cautious, devious
but persevering steps, extremely laborious and

mystifying.' Even so late as November 1917 he declared in the House of Commons :

'I am utterly opposed to that suggestion [a Generalissimo]. It would not work. It would produce real friction, and might produce not merely friction between the armies, but friction between the nations and the Governments.'

Inexorable circumstances—not Mr. Lloyd George —raised Foch, ' a week ago described as a " dotard," ' to the supreme command at Doullens on March 26, 1918.

The year 1916 opened in gloom. The Russians had suffered a series of heavy defeats, Bulgaria had entered the war, and Serbia had been overrun. General Townshend's force was imprisoned at Kut, and the relic of the Dardanelles expedition still lingered in a position of much danger at Helles. The failure of this great venture was, in Mr. Churchill's view, ' fatal to Lord Kitchener ' ![1] Moltke had gone under, and on February 21, 1916, Falkenhayn began his terrific attack on Verdun, which throughout the year largely ruled the course of the Western campaign. The threat to the vital Mezières-Thionville railway may have influenced him ; but Mr. Churchill considers that this momentous decision was a German mistake of the first class, and that the French, by whom the retention of this old and dismantled fortress was treated as a point of honour,

' would have been wise to play with the Germans

[1] It might fairly be argued that this misconceived venture might have been ' fatal ' to Mr. Churchill.

around Verdun, economising their forces as much as possible . . . and endeavouring to lead their enemies into a pocket or other unfavourable position.'

Space fails to discuss this and other facile and highly disputable imaginings. The series of great battles on the Somme are admirably described ; but Mr. Churchill, in accordance with the views he consistently upholds, underrates the effects obtained at heavy cost. The mass attacks on the Somme were not far from success, and it is Ludendorff who declared that the decline of the military might of Germany dates from 1916, when, as he says, ' we were completely exhausted on the Western Front.' If, as Mr. Churchill admits, ' never again did the mass of German rank and file fight as they fought on the Somme,' the cruel sacrifices of the Allied armies were not all in vain. Nevertheless, in a long Memorandum of August, 1916, circulated to the Cabinet,[1] and in his text, he reaches a ' sombre verdict,' and criticisms are abundant. It is pleasanter to turn to his fine tribute to Kitchener's Army of which the ' battlefields of the Somme were the graveyards.' Nowhere else is his mastery of forceful English more worthily or more effectively employed.

The time has not yet come for an impartial judgment, in this country at least, on the causes of the most momentous failure in our naval history. Four years elapsed after the Battle of Jutland before the movements of Admiral Scheer at the critical

---

[1] By Sir F. Smith, now Lord Birkenhead.

period were understood, and fictions thus arose and became deep-rooted. The earlier diagrams of the manœuvres of the fleets were most misleading, and the evolution, which the High Seas Fleet had sedulously practised, was held to be impracticable by our naval authorities long after it had been successfully carried out in action three times by the German command. Mr. Churchill's views, expressed three months after the event, were precise and dogmatic. ' There was,' he wrote, ' no strategic cause ' impelling us to fight off the Danish coast. ' What harm does it do us if the German Fleet takes a promenade at sea ? ' To him, therefore, it then appeared that ' naval history records no prouder assertion of fighting superiority on the part of the stronger fleet ' than the abortive action of May 31, 1916. He now describes this action with a wealth of detail, and he finds much to criticise.

In a sense, the issue may be said to have been predetermined by two untoward conditions. In the first place, the structural defects of Lord Fisher's battle cruisers helped to rob Sir D. Beatty of a decisive victory over Admiral Hipper's squadron, when he reached an interposing position with a force, nominally at least, far superior to that of his antagonist, for whom escape was apparently impossible. If the four ' Queen Elizabeths ' had been in company with the Battle Cruiser Fleet when the action began, a smashing blow might still have been delivered ; but grave defects in signalling arrangements appeared on other occasions, as Rear-Admiral Harper records, and the blame which Mr. Churchill imputes to Rear-Admiral Evan-Thomas for the unfortunate delay in bringing the 5th Battle Squadron into action is not deserved.

The German battle cruisers were able to find the range and to get hits more quickly than our own,[1] and the destruction of the *Indefatigable* and *Queen Mary*, with the hair-breadth escape of the *Lion*, occurred in the first half-hour. Mr. Churchill considers that at shorter ranges our heavier shells would have shown relatively to better advantage. Incidentally, Admiral Beatty's opening action raises the whole vexed question of the policy of building battle cruisers with weak armour and ammunition hoists unprotected against a downward flash. The ruling idea was that these very fast ships, with a much heavier armament than that of their German analogues, would be able to select long ranges and to injure their opponents with a minimum of risk. Experience pointed to a different conclusion. Mr. Churchill tells us that he 'recoiled from the battle cruiser type' in 1911, as did some reasoned naval opinion. What happened in the battle cruiser engagement was thus largely due to prior causes. Structural defects in this new type of warship caused the loss of more than 3300 officers and men in the three vessels sunk by explosion.

In the second place, Admiral Sir J. Jellicoe had laid down in advance his general tactical procedure in the event of a fleet action, and had explained his reasons for extreme caution. In a most im-

---

[1] They had, however, an advantage in visibility at this time.

portant letter to the Admiralty of October 30, 1914, he pointed out *inter alia* that

'The Germans have shown that they rely to a very great extent on submarines, mines, and torpedoes, and there can be no doubt whatever that they will endeavour to make the fullest use of these weapons in a fleet action, especially since they possess an actual superiority in these particular directions.'

As the Germans could not rely on using submarines or mines except ' in waters selected by them and in the southern area of the North Sea, my object will, therefore, be to fight the fleet action in the northern portion of the North Sea.' He then proceeded to explain how the German submarines might be expected to be used, the idea being to lead the Grand Fleet on to a prepared battle area.

' If, for instance, the enemy battle fleet were to turn away from an advancing fleet, I should assume that the intention was to draw us over mines and submarines and should decline to be so drawn. I desire particularly to draw the attention of their Lordships to this point, since it may be deemed a refusal of battle, and indeed might possibly result in failure to bring the enemy to action as soon as is expected and hoped. . . .[1] It is quite within the bounds of possibility that half of our battle fleet might be disabled by under-water attack before the

[1] It does not seem to have been realised that, if a retreating fleet were not followed up, a naval victory might become impossible.

guns opened fire at all, if a false move is made.'

This momentous document was approved by Mr. Churchill; but he does ' not accept on behalf of the Board of Admiralty any responsibility for the actual conduct ' of the Battle of Jutland eighteen months later when the Grand Fleet had been powerfully reinforced. The responsibilities of the Commander-in-Chief were undoubtedly tremendous; but ' praiseworthy precaution had induced a defensive habit of mind and a scheme of tactics which hampered the Grand Fleet even when the special conditions enjoining caution did not exist.'

The exaggerated fear of torpedo attack at long ranges had been effectively exposed, just before the outbreak of war, by Admiral Sir Reginald N. Custance as a result of a careful analysis of the war performances of the under-water weapon. The battle area of May 31 could not have been prepared in advance. No submarines were present, for the sufficient reasons which Admiral Scheer has given. We had a marked superiority in torpedo craft, and our torpedoes did more destruction than those of the Germans, while the only minefield trap, by which the *Ostfriesland* was damaged, was laid by Admiral Jellicoe.[1] The officially approved tactical scheme, however, ruled the

---

[1] In addition, three submarines left Harwich at 7 a.m. on May 30 for the Horns Reef Passage with orders to lie on the bottom till June 2. The change in the situation was not communicated to them, ' although there seems no reason why this should not have been done.' They, therefore, carried out their original orders, thereby missing a good opportunity, (Admiral Harper, *The Truth about Jutland*). The German Fleet must have passed over them.

course of the battle, and saved the German Fleet at the most critical moment. The issue was predetermined, and some of Mr. Churchill's criticisms go wide of the mark. He dwells on what he regards as three lost opportunities, and among the purple patches such an appalling sentence as ' Three times is a lot ' comes as a shock. A difference of reckoning between the Grand and the Battle Cruiser Fleet, amounting to 11 miles,[1] and lack of precise information—due mainly to want of system—placed Admiral Jellicoe in a dilemma when actual contact with the High Seas Fleet was imminent. Mr. Churchill critically discusses the deployment, completed at 6.38 p.m., by which time Admiral Scheer had turned his command ' together ' and was retiring, and he explains at length the advantages of a different evolution. It is true that the cruising formation of the Grand Fleet was maintained far too long.[2] An earlier deployment, bringing that fleet into order of battle with its scouts and flotillas in their proper positions, might have provided the first of Mr. Churchill's ' chances ; ' but the delay was due to the fact that the bearing of the enemy's fleet was not accurately known. As carried out, the deployment of the battleships was in part under fire. There was local ' bunching,' and much disorder of the scouting forces, leading to considerable losses. There was no time, even if it had been possible, to give the necessary orders

---

[1] This might have been anticipated in the circumstances—dead reckoning and much zigzagging.
[2] The presence and course of the High Seas Fleet were signalled to the flagship from the *Southampton* at 4.38 p.m., and at 6.15 p.m. the deployment began ; but previously, at 3.13 p.m., the columns of battleships had been opened out in preparation for deployment.

to the scattered squadrons and flotillas when the enemy was close at hand, and the Grand Fleet thus obtained contact in disadvantageous conditions.

Yet a real chance was to be given. Admiral Scheer again turned his fleet 'together' to attack the Grand Fleet fully deployed, and to place himself in a position of grave danger.[1] As he has explained, ' The manœuvre would be bound to surprise the enemy, and if the blow fell heavily, it would facilitate the breaking loose at night.'[2] Two German flotillas delivered an attack, and the Grand Fleet turned away according to plan, and lost the enemy, never again to obtain contact. This was the real crisis of the Battle of Jutland, and the main reason why the most powerful fleet the world has ever seen was never brought into effective action.

Mr. Churchill selects as his third chance the moment when Admiral Jellicoe received at about 11.30 p.m. the Admiralty message announcing that the German Battle Fleet had been ordered back to port at 9.14 p.m. on a course stated, which indicated the Horns Reef Passage. If the Admiral had decided to act on this important information, he had, according to his critic, ' only to turn his fleet on to a course parallel to the Germans in order to make sure of bringing them to action at

[1] ' It [the High Seas Fleet] was now heading straight into the centre of the arc formed by the British Fleet. In a few minutes the leading squadron and battle cruisers would be threatened with envelopment and the concentrated fire of practically the whole Grand Fleet ' (Admiralty Official Narrative).

[2] Admiral Harper describes this manœuvre as a ' blundering ' attack but it was bold, extremely astute, well executed, and perfectly successful for Admiral Scheer's purpose.

daybreak.' This can only be regarded as a rash speculation. The Grand Fleet had been turned nearly south at 9 p.m. and was proceeding at 17 knots. The 1st Battle Squadron was not in station, and as the *Marlborough* had been hit by a torpedo and the flag had not at once been transferred, this squadron became detached.[1] The Commander-in-Chief could not know the positions of his scouting forces. He had ordered the flotillas to follow five miles astern without instructions, and the whole German Fleet crashed through them in the darkness. Thus prolonged fortuitous fighting occurred, in which our young officers displayed conspicuous gallantry and initiative. The position of the enemy was not understood, and a night action could not be risked by the Grand Fleet for the reasons given in Admiral Jellicoe's Report :

' The German organisation for night is very good. Their system of recognition signals is excellent. Ours is practically *nil*. Their search-lights are superior to ours, and they use them with great effect. Finally, their method of firing at night gives excellent results.'

These reasons, if humiliating, were certainly cogent. After the crucial turn away, not followed by a determined attempt to find out where the enemy was, the decision to steer south can easily be justified. The Grand Fleet could not, in any case, have been ready to fight at daybreak because, as a whole, it was not in hand, and time would have been needed to bring it into order of battle.

---

[1] She did not rejoin the Grand Fleet till the evening of June 1.

Mr. Churchill's general conclusions are that there were chances on May 31 and later on August 19

' for gripping the enemy without in any way increasing the risk of being led into an under-water trap. A more flexible system of fleet training and manœuvring would have enabled these movements to be made.[1] The attempt to centralise in a single hand the whole conduct in action of so vast a fleet failed.'

This may be admitted ; but shortly after the battle Mr. Churchill's imagination led him to fancy the heaven-born commander ' regulating almost by gesture from moment to moment the course of the supreme and intense battle '—an attractive picture far removed from the possibilities of war. There are some inevitable drawbacks to the writing of naval history by an ex-First Lord. Captain Frothingham's able study of the Battle of Jutland has the great merit of detachment, and he explains why ' the ensuing results of the British failure to win a decisive victory at Jutland became more and more disastrous to the Entente Allies as time went on.'

He attributes this failure to the ' cautious policy,' the ' defensive idea,' approved by the Admiralty, and his verdict is that the ' ill-effects should not solely be charged against the men who were fighting the battle.'[2] In this country controversy will continue to rage, and Mr. Churchill has given it a fresh impulse. Perhaps in the future

[1] The working of a large fleet by divisions had been suggested and tried by Sir R. N. Custance and Admiral of the Fleet Sir W. May, but apparently did not commend itself to the Admiralty.
[2] *The Naval History of the War*, Vol. II (Cambridge Harvard University Press, 1925).

the tragedy of Jutland will take its true place in the history of the Great War, and it will be realised that psychological causes pre-existing made a Nelson or a Togo victory impossible. The personnel of the Grand Fleet was incomparable. From the Commander-in-Chief to the youngest boy, all were intent on a decision ; but defensive ideals had for some years prevailed at the Admiralty, where monster ships and guns had seemed more important than the study of war. It followed that, on the day of trial, the High Seas Fleet, with a great inferiority in numbers, gun-power, and speed, proved to be better prepared than our own in important respects.[1]

It remains a popular delusion that the German Fleet did not again show itself in the North Sea, and Mr. Churchill has done well to describe in detail the instructive evolutions on August 18, when again this Fleet, less the slow 2nd Battle Squadron, was at sea with a definite plan, and again there was the chance of a fleet action. Two pieces of false information prevented contact. The light cruiser *Nottingham* was torpedoed by a submarine ; but a mine-field trap being suspected, the Grand Fleet was turned about and lost four hours in its movement south. Later, Admiral Scheer received a false report from an airship that strong British forces—the Harwich flotilla which was taken for the Grand Fleet—had been seen to the southward, and fearing to be cut off, he returned to port.

---

[1] If it is necessary to find scapegoats, they must be sought in the archives of the Admiralty. In 1892, the writer gave a plain warning of what might follow from a warped naval policy.

The year 1916 reached its 'crimson close,' and 1917—crucial because of the Russian *débâcle* and the intervention of America—was to see a repetition of the offensive policy in the West against which Mr. Churchill consistently inveighs. A local success at Verdun, carried out mainly by General Mangin, had brought a new exponent of the art of war into prominence, and 'forthwith a stream of celebrities took the road to Verdun and made for the first time acquaintance' with General Nivelle, who had become Commander-in-Chief of the armies of France on December 12, superseding Foch, Pétain, and Castelnau. His 'forceful and continuous argument,' spoken in English, captivated Mr. Lloyd George and led to a 'promise,' not communicated to Haig or Robertson, of control over the British forces, which naturally created difficulties. The new strategy was to depend on surprise and, in Nivelle's words, on 'violence, brutality, and rapidity.' Mr. Churchill lucidly explains the vitiation of the assumed conditions by Ludendorff's sudden withdrawal and the other causes which led to a great failure. On May 15, 1917, Nivelle was dismissed, and it fell to Pétain to render invaluable service by restoring the *moral* and discipline of the French armies, grievously shaken by the 'experiment' which our and many French generals had viewed from the first with misgivings unshared by Mr. Lloyd George. The prolongation of the attack at Paschendaele, attributed to the 'Haig-Robertson combination,' is severely condemned. The cost may well seem excessive ; but the natural desire of the British generals to occupy the enemy during the critical period of Pétain's labours, and the fact that Sir D. Haig ultimately succeeded in occupying a strong position, might have received recognition.

On July 22, Mr. Churchill conveyed his views to the Prime Minister.

'With regard to the East, the truth is staring us in the face. An army of six divisions . . . should be taken from the Salonica Front and put in behind Jemal's army. This will force that army to surrender, and all the allied troops in Syria and Palestine, including Allenby's, would be free by the spring of next year for action in Italy or France.'

Mr. Lloyd George's response was to offer the command in Palestine to General Smuts, who declined it because his stipulations were not accepted, and General Allenby proceeded to smash Jemal, and in a masterly campaign to drive the Turkish army before him and to occupy Jerusalem. This fine offensive wins Mr. Churchill's unstinted praise.

In July 1917 he became Minister of Munitions, and we have an impressive account of the vast activities of his department, which, later, was preparing on a tremendous scale for the 'unfought campaign' of 1919. Yet the almost overwhelming responsibilities thus involved did not suffice, and he was constantly in France watching great battles and occupying a 'central position between the Army and the War Cabinet.'

Before the end of 1917, German intrigue,

crowned by the sinister mission of Lenin and his myrmidons, had secured the total collapse of the great Russian armies, which at the beginning of the year were better equipped than ever before. In October the ' astounding disaster ' at Caporetto occurred, and heavy detachment from the armies in France was needed to re-establish the Italian Front. Meanwhile Ludendorff was busily engaged in transferring divisions from the East to the West and in maturing the ' Michaels ' and the ' Mars ' plans for a mass attack. American forces in large numbers could not be available for many months, and over the High Commands in France brooded the menace of their greatest peril.[1]

'The cry for a new offensive died away. The mood swung round to pure defence—and against heavy odds. It was a revolution at once silent and complete. I responded to it with instant relief.'

Nevertheless, Mr. Churchill blames Sir W. Robertson for the inadequate reinforcement of our armies, which nearly led to disaster.

'He succeeded in enforcing his policy against the better judgment of successive Cabinets and War Councils, with the result that when he left the War Office in February 1918, the British and French armies were at their weakest strength and fighting power.'

[1] ' Numerically,' wrote Ludendorff of the time when his concentration in the West was completed, ' we had never been so strong in comparison with our enemies,' and he has recently explained that, by March 1918, he had brought more than 480,000 German troops from Russia, Rumania, and Italy to the Western Front (*New York American*, May 22, 1927).

The Field-Marshal has explained the earnest efforts of the military authorities to obtain reinforcements ; but Mr. Lloyd George believed that we were ' over-insured in the West,'[1] and according to Mr. Churchill, he

> ' did not feel that, if the troops were once in France, he would be strong enough to resist those military pressures for an offensive which had so often overborne the wiser judgment of Statesmen.'

And yet we are told that military judgment had ' swung round to pure defence ' ! The result of the Prime Minister's doubt of his powers was the overwhelming of our 5th Army and a heavy handicap in the ' fearful year which was approaching.'

Mr. Churchill is at his best in describing the course of ' the mightiest military conception and the most terrific onslaught which the annals of war record.' His chapters dealing with Ludendorff's smashing blows delivered against our armies during forty days and at length parried, with the tremendous attacks on the French, based upon the surprise on the Chemin des Dames on May 27 and pressed beyond the Marne, and with the ' turn of the tide,' when the stricken forces of the Allies swept back the German hordes and won a final and crushing victory, are admirable. The prolonged ordeal of the splendid troops of France and Britain, and of their sorely-tried commanders, could

---

[1] There were at this time nearly 760,000 troops in the East (Sir W. Robertson).

not be more impressively portrayed. Ludendorff's tremendous effort, which Mr. Churchill unsparingly condemns, was nearly justified by success, which the American Army,[1] just in time to act with vigour and to hearten the war-worn forces of the Allies, rendered impossible. But for the fortitude of the British soldier and the devotion of the French *poilu*, which by the end of July had stemmed the ' most terrific onslaught ' in the annals of war, what might not have happened ? General Mangin's flanking counterstroke on July 18, in which ' two strong American divisions ' took part,[2] and General Rawlinson's brilliantly successful attack on August 8 marked the beginning of the ebb-tide. Henceforth gloom settled down upon the German Headquarters.

At the end of August the Cabinet sent an amazing message to Sir D. Haig warning him against the losses which a great offensive might involve— a message well calculated to shake the determination of a weak commander. It is pleasant to find that Mr. Churchill realises that our General had a ' truer view ' of the situation than the ' national leaders.' But this significant admission is marred by a reiterated condemnation of the ' obstinacy and serene confidence ' of Foch and Haig, who devised and carried out the measures which led in a few months to complete victory, while as late as

[1] What we owe to the fact that General Pershing from the first realised the gravity of the situation and that the American Government, therefore, made preparations on a vast scale has been inadequately recognised.

[2] Mr. Churchill fails to bring out the fact that, as Marshal Foch has pointed out, there were five American divisions, 'which on July 18th, participated in the victorious counter offensive of the 10th and 6th French armies, between the Aisne and the Marne, contributing notably to victory.' This part of the narrative shows signs of carelessness.

September 5 Mr. Churchill was still contemplating the ' unfought campaign ' of 1919.

As historian, Mr. Churchill suffers from a natural desire to record the prominent and often valuable part which his vigorous personality played in council, from a too exalted estimate of ' the wiser judgment of Statesmen,' and from a super-abundance of speculative criticism. He has given us pictures of war which can fearlessly challenge comparison with those of Napier and of Tolstoy. As a vivid narrative of a long sequence of tremendous events, his book will not be surpassed. Valuable material of many kinds has been brought together and lucidly recorded. The chapters entitled ' The Munitions Budget ' and ' Britain Conquers the U-Boats ' embody permanent contributions to history. If, as I have ventured to point out, his analysis of cause and effect and his attribution of blame to some of the actors in the great tragedy are not always just, this arises from personal bias uncorrected by adequate study of the past, and from a natural combativeness which supplies the spice that will attract a large section of readers.

That the Great War was in many respects gravely mismanaged, partly by reason of the inherent disabilities of our form of democracy[1] for the conduct of war, cannot be denied ; but it may be that the huge scale of operations, and the difficulty of balancing the advantages and disadvantages of widely separated yet interdependent

[1] In America, no injurious conflict between the ' Statesmen ' and General Pershing seems to have arisen in regard to the huge military preparations begun in 1917.

plans were beyond the capacity of the human brain. The great political lessons, bearing upon the supreme direction of operations so complex, are best conveyed in the measured pages of Sir W. Robertson's revealing book, which serves as a needed corrective to many passages in Mr. Churchill's always fascinating volumes.

CHAPTER II

THE GERMAN LOSSES ON THE SOMME
JULY-DECEMBER, 1916

BY SIR CHARLES OMAN, M.P.,
Chichele Professor of Modern History at Oxford

THE appearance of the Chancellor of the Exchequer's solid volumes dealing with the 'World Crisis' has led to a revival of many old controversies concerning details of the Great War by land and sea, and to the starting of one or two new ones. Discussion has ranged from that general problem as to the relative importance of the Eastern and the Western Fronts on which every student has a right to his own opinion, down to technical matters of naval tactics, on which only naval men have a right to criticise each other's views.

My own main interest in the book comes from its containing two chapters—mainly strategical in character—on which one who was immersed in statistics from morn to eve, during two years of the Great War, feels bound to make his comment, lest certain figures should pass undisputed, and deductions from them should grow into generally accepted truisms. These are the chapters on the 'Blood Test' and the 'Battle of the Somme'— sixty pages of closely reasoned and most interesting controversy. With their bearings on the general thesis of the book I shall have little to do. But it seems to me that many of the basic tables of statistics, on which that main thesis rests, need investigation and revision.

Now no one will dispute that the Battle of the Somme is a terrible memory—only less terrible than the memory of the offensive of the following year, which, starting at Arras, finally died down in the mud and blood of Paschendaele. The offensive of 1917 was longer, and more costly by some 130,000 casualties, than that of 1916; but in all its months there was no single day so deadly to the British Army as the 1st of July of the earlier year, when fifteen gallant divisions flung themselves against the long German trench-line that stretched from Gommecourt to Maricourt and failed to break in, save on one comparatively short section at the south end of the hostile front. That day cost the assailants something like 50,000 casualties: the remembrance of its slaughter is still heavy on the minds of all who can recall its first impression. And four months of fighting only a few degrees less costly were to follow, till we had bought an irregular scrap of ground twelve miles long by seven miles deep at the price of something approaching 350,000 killed, wounded, and missing—not to speak of the very considerable losses of our French Allies at the south end of the battle line.

Now Mr. Winston Churchill's deduction from these deplorable figures is that while we were suffering so heavily we were inflicting no corresponding punishment upon the Germans. On page 51 of his first volume he puts the casualties of the British at 481,842, and those of the enemy at only 236,194. The latter figure, however obtained, is (as I shall show) much less than half of the total German loss upon the Somme between July and November. And the total casualties of the British and French Armies really work out, not at a 2 to 1 proportion, but as a little less heavy than those of the enemy. The figures are lamentable enough, but at least let us get them correct. And then the deduction from them as to the meaning of the Somme battles may be somewhat different from that drawn in the *World Crisis.*

What no reader of that most interesting work would, I think, realise is that all through those dreadful five months the Germans, far from opposing us with inferior forces, and suffering losses not half so great as ours, were being hit no less hard than the Allies, and were thrusting into the great *mêlée* on the Somme, one after another, every available unit that they possessed on the Western Front which was considered fit to stand the strain. They emerged from it with 50 per cent, 60 per cent, even 70 per cent losses, and were sent to the rear in rotation, to be out of action for months, while the skeleton cadres were being refilled with recruits. Some reappeared after a long interval with a new personnel, others were relegated for good to quiet fronts, or even sent to Russia, where the highest military qualities were not required in the German front line.

A wholly unfair effect is produced on pages 176–79 of the *World Crisis,* where the awful losses of our 8th Division on the first day of the Somme battle—5500 of all ranks—are contrasted with the comparative immunity of one German regiment, the 180th, which, though in the front line, lost under 300 officers and men in its three battalions. Such a comparison is, of course, deceptive. The figures of the 8th Division ought, in common fairness, to be placed parallel to those of a German unit which fared badly on the bloody 1st of July, not to those of one which was fortunate. A very different effect on the reader's mind is left if we cite, not the figures of the 180th Regiment, but those of its near neighbour in the line, the 111th Reserve Infantry Regiment, only about a mile away, which was taken out of the front by the enemy at the earliest possible moment, and sent to the rear reporting 1850 casualties in its three battalions out of 2700 present,—no less gloomy a record than that of our 8th Division ; the whole of this loss was suffered on July 1 alone. Clearly the 180th had exceptional luck and should not be quoted as a typical case.

I may cite another equally deceptive comparison made on page 51 of the *World Crisis*. We are shown figures purporting to prove that the British loss in officers on the Somme was four times that of the Germans—21,974 to 4879. A footnote does indeed remark that German commissioned officers were 'less numerous' per battalion than British. But who would guess from this note that in July 1916 we were sending into the line battalions with twenty-five combatant officers or more—the Germans battalions with only ten or eleven?[1] For by

---

[1] Not including, of course, adjutants, paymasters, transport officers, etc., on the staff of the regiment.

this stage of the war the places of a great proportion of the original commissioned officers in a German unit were being supplied by ' *offizier-stellvertreter*' —' substitute officers ' who were in theory non-commissioned officers only. Having looked over many German regimental histories, which describe individual battle incidents, I can vouch for the fact that in very many German battalions half the platoons were at this time in charge of ' substitutes,' and that a company was lucky if it had three regular officers to lead it. To make a fair comparison of officer casualties we ought to reckon on the German side all the N.C.O.'s discharging officers' functions, and if this were done the proportion of losses on the two sides would be not far from equal. In the German casualty lists, when totals and percentages are added up, it always appears that the proportion of officers killed, wounded, or missing is not much over 2 per cent of the total losses of all ranks. This does not mean that they were told to spare themselves, but that there were not more than 2 per cent of commissioned officers in the fighting companies of the unit—the duties of officers being discharged by N.C.O.'s to an extent of which we had at the time little conception. Hence an unjust criticism sometimes made on the paucity of casualties in the commissioned ranks of the German Army : they exposed themselves freely, but were not numerous.

Turning back to the general topic of German losses on the Somme, we must remember that in July–November 1916 a normal German Army

Corps had eighteen infantry battalions—not the twenty-four with which it started the war. The Jäger battalions originally attached to the active divisions, were nearly all taken away and utilized elsewhere in the earliest period of the war. I give, therefore, 24 battalions only as the original strength. Then from most brigades one three-battalion regiment had been deducted, to make up the so-called 'reconstituted divisions,' with new and high divisional numbers, all of which had only three regiments and nine battalions. The infantry, therefore, of an army corps was now no more than 18,000 strong, and of a division no more than 9000 strong, if the cadres had been duly and recently filled up with drafts. But many units were not in this happy condition, having been hurried up from some distant part of the Western Front without full completion of their numbers, because they were so urgently required on the Somme that prompt appearance was more important than numerical completeness.

Now the German Front against which the Allied attack was directed on July 1–5 was held by nineteen divisions, of which thirteen had been on the spot on the first two days of the battle, while the other six were hurried up on or before July 5. It may be worth while to give in detail the losses of those original holders of the German line, in order that the reader may appreciate the fact that it was not British units alone which were suffering devastating casualties. The troops in line on July 1–2 were :

2nd Guard Reserve Division . .	5,982
11th Division ⎫ forming VI Corps .	
12th Division ⎭	16,688
11th Reserve Division ⎫ forming VI	
12th Reserve Division ⎭ Reserve Corps	14,811
26th Reserve Division ⎫ forming XIV	
28th Reserve Division ⎭ Reserve Corps	16,488
36th Division (of XVII Corps) . .	4,027
52nd Division	5,906
111th ' Reconstituted Division ' .	4,002
121st ' Reconstituted Division ' .	6,278
10th Bavarian Division . . .	5,644
5th Bavarian Reserve Division . .	4,036
Total . .	83,872

I do not, of course, say that all these 83,000
casualties of the original German front line troops
on the Somme were suffered in the first five days
of the battle, nor that they should be deducted
only from the 117,000 men who would have been
engaged if each of the 117 battalions in question
had been able to put 1000 men in line, which we
know that they could not. That would imply a
70 per cent loss all round, and a 90 per cent loss
in some cases, such as the VI and XIV Reserve
Corps. But some of these divisions were kept in
the front line for many days after July 1–5 and
received drafts, while others were withdrawn,
rested, refilled, and sent into the line again in
October or November. And the main losses of
some of them (e.g. the 5th Bavarian Reserve Divi-

sion) are known to have been suffered at dates later than the early days of July. But undoubtedly the first-comers to the Somme fighting were hit no less hard than their British and French opponents. The 121st Division, taken out of the line as early as was possible, reported 6278 casualties in the opening days, was sent to the rear at once, recruited, and despatched to Russia as incapable of Western Front fighting any longer. The 123rd Division, which reached the front on July 5, was withdrawn before July 12 with 4402 casualties and sent to Russia also. Of the 14,811 casualties of the VI Reserve Corps—original troops of July 1–2—we know that at least 12,000 belong to the first days of the Somme battle : of the 5048 casualties of the 185th Division, which came up on July 5 and was gone by July 12, we know that 4000 date from its earliest appearance in the line.

Nor did the divisions which arrived at a later date than July 5 suffer less than their fellows. There were in line before the end of the month of July :

	Casualties reported
3rd Guard Reserve Division (sent to Russia in August) . . .	5,010
7th Division ⎱ forming IV Corps . 8th Division ⎰	17,147
5th Division (of III Corps) . .	7,794
44th Reserve Division (of XXII Reserve Corps)	8,625
183rd Division	6,833
17th Division ⎱ forming IX Corps . 18th Division ⎰	17,289

beside eleven other divisions which did not report quite such annihilating losses, though none of them (I think) registered, first and last, less than 4000 casualties.

Of units arriving in August on the Somme :

17th Reserve Division } forming IX		
18th Reserve Division } Reserve Corps	16,114	
26th Division } forming XIII Corps .	10,100	
27th Division }		
Guard Corps (1st and 2nd Divisions)	11,480	
4th Guard Division . . .	6,298	
23rd Reserve Division } forming XII Saxon Reserve	15,543	
32nd Reserve Division } Corps		
8th Bavarian Division . . .	6,429	
3rd Bavarian Division } forming II	12,307	
4th Bavarian Division } Bavarian Corps		

besides five other divisions which suffered less than 50 per cent losses, though none (I think) less than 35 or 40 per cent over.

And so matters went on till November, new combatants being drawn from every corner of the Western Front, till something like 100 divisions in all had been put through the mill. Some went in only once ; some, having been rested and recruited, being withdrawn in July or August, were back again at the front in October and November. I note that of the thirteen divisions which had held the line on July 1–2, four were again on the Somme in the end of the year, three had been sent to Russia by September, and six were resting on quiet (or comparatively quiet) portions of the French Front.

The system of the Germans in reporting losses in their official *Verlustliste*, which appeared almost daily, was to start in each number with the losses of the senior regiment which had sent in a report lately, and to go down numerically through the units, till the last name of some small technical corps or labour battalion had been reached. Thus of three successive regiments whose casualties appeared one after another in the *Verlustliste* of one day the first might be in Russia, the second in Alsace, and the third opposite Ypres. It was obviously the purpose of the editors of these lists to mix up losses on all possible fronts, in order that their readers in the calculating bureaux of Paris or London might be given as much trouble as possible in collecting useful statistics. So the casualties of a single regiment were dropped about in many successive numbers of the *Verlustliste*— those of five companies (perhaps) appearing on the first day of the month, those of three others on the fifth day, those of the remaining four on the tenth. And this was still more the case with simultaneous losses in a brigade or division : sometimes in a three-regiment division, engaged on a definite day, all the casualties of two of the regiments might be printed at one place or another in the lists of (let us say) September 1 to September 6, but those of the third regiment might not begin to appear till September 25 or even October 1. It was quite possible, as I know from personal experience, for the calculator in London or Paris to say, ' We know that the xyth Division was heavily engaged on August 1—we have losses of regiments a and c of it amounting to 1000 each, but none of regiment b, though it is now a fortnight since we counted the last names of regiment c. Regiment b must send in its casualties soon, and they will probably not be less than 1000 also : perhaps they will be a good many more, the heaviest sufferer having been reserved for the last printing.' This sort of calculation was invariably justified by the appearance of the belated statistics within a few days. The main difficulty of the compiler was to keep up an accurate account of the arrival and departure of German divisions on the particular front whose statistics were under his charge. But information at the War Office was wonderfully good and prompt.

The only real difficulty that occurred in counting the Somme casualties was that the Germans used two extemporised divisions and two other extemporised brigades named after their commanders, Generals Liebert and Franke, Osten and Scholz, which consisted of stray battalions (or in some cases regiments) drawn from different units and hastily thrown together. When the identity of one of these battalions (or regiments) was established it was rather natural to assume that the rest of the regiment (or division) to which the detected unit belonged had arrived on the Somme. It took some time to discover, e.g. that though the 100th and 125th Regiments (both under Franke) had arrived, this did not mean that the whole of the 23rd and 26th Divisions to which they belonged respectively, had yet reached the front—though both ultimately did so. Liebert's 'group' of thirteen miscellaneous battalions opposite the French was a specially tiresome problem. However, such difficulties were always solved in the end.

The casualties which the Germans kept reporting from the Somme were progressively printed with longer and longer intervals between the day on which the casualty occurred and the day on which it was acknowledged in print. By November as much as four or five weeks intervened. The acknowledged totals had got up to about 420,000 for the infantry alone by the end of the November *Verlustliste*, when the large majority of the losses of that month had not yet been printed. Then, in the first days of December 1916, the Berlin office suddenly 'shut down' and published no more regimental lists. The reason was obvious—the total was getting too ghastly, and the information afforded to the Paris or London calculator was too valuable.

From December 6 onward the system adopted was to publish every day only alphabetical lists of individuals, from A to Z, with no indication of the unit to which any man belonged. Those who fell on the Russian or Balkan front were mixed in with those who fell in France or Belgium. No further information as to regimental casualties was obtainable save by methods more circuitous and difficult than that of merely compiling the totals of the *Verlustliste*.

What were the missing November losses? We know that many late-arriving divisions, which only came into the front line in October or November, had but a small fraction of their losses acknowledged. By December units known to have been deeply engaged in the desperate fighting on the Ancre about Beaumont Hamel, etc., in November had not yet printed any losses at all, and units withdrawn to the rear as exhausted (e.g. the Marine Division and the Bavarian I Corps), which had only turned up for the October fighting, had but just commenced to dribble in their first casualties when the *Verlustliste* ceased to print regimental figures.[1] I cannot put the unacknowledged German infantry losses, which had not been published by November 30, at less than 60,000—a figure much smaller than those actually published in any of the months of August, September, October, November, from the Somme Front, in two of which the totals came to well over 100,000 casualties per month, in the third to 100,000, and in the fourth to nearly 80,000.

The whole therefore works out as :

Infantry losses acknowledged in the *Verlustliste* down to end of November, as shown in the table at end of this chapter, about   .   .   . 420,000
Unacknowledged infantry losses for late October and November .   .   .   60,000
Losses July–November of artillery, engineers, pioneers, sappers, train, technical troops, labour battalions,

---

[1] By December 1 the two divisions of the I Bavarian Corps had only printed 1900 casualties out of their 18,000 infantry ; yet they are known to have been withdrawn, absolutely exhausted, before November was over.

and other auxiliary units, at least   50,000
(a most moderate estimate, for many
engineer companies and artillery
batteries were annihilated).

Total . . 530,000

It must be remembered that we have 420,000 casualties recorded with the name and rank of every man killed and wounded in the infantry alone, without adding anything either for the auxiliary arms or for the losses still unpublished at the moment when the *Verlustliste* ceased to appear in their original form.

How then are we to deal with the latest statement from the *Reichsarchiv* that the total losses on the Somme *for all arms* were only 436,651 ? I can only submit the following observations. These German figures give for the whole period from July to November :

Killed or missing 164,055
Wounded .   . 272,596=436,651 in all.

Now the number of prisoners taken by the Allies during these months was 83,655. Deducting this figure from the 164,055 ' killed or missing ' we obtain a total of 80,400 for the killed.

But the proportion of 80,000 killed to 272,000 wounded, i.e. 3·4 wounded only for each man killed, seems to be an impossible one. It gives far too low a proportion of wounded. For the British official figures for the number of men wounded to every fatal casualty are not 3·4 to 1 but 4½ to 1.[1] And French statistics show, when lightly

[1] Statistics of *The Military Effort of the British Empire*, p. 246.

wounded are included, much the same proportion, while the proportion in the American Army was over 5 to 1. Is it credible that the Allied shells and bullets were so much more deadly than the German, that they killed men outright with an accuracy superior in the proportion of $4\frac{1}{2}$ to 3.4? This seems an absurd hypothesis—and the only way out of the problem is to suppose that while the British figures (as we know) give every recorded casualty, however slight, the German revised estimates do not. Indeed, they produce figures incompatible with the *Verlustliste*. If the effect of the fire on each side was more or less equal, the German lists should show not 272,000 wounded but about 360,000. And adding the 80,000 dead and the 83,000 prisoners we get 523,000, a sum very nearly approaching the 530,000 which I have indicated above as the total that can be deduced from the losses recorded in the *Verlustliste*, with the hypothetical addition of unrecorded losses. And what were the corresponding losses on the side of the British and the French? Decidedly less, as far as I can make out, than those of their adversaries.

The British official totals for casualties in the whole Somme fighting from July 1 to November 18 are :

4th Army	277,134
5th Army	57,681
3rd Army (on July 1–2 only)	7,847
	342,662

[The 3rd Army only engaged in the first general assault its southernmost divisions, and did not take any further part in the battles of the succeeding months.]

The French official totals, from the return of the 6th Army, come to 146,672, of which casualties 44,308 were 'slightly wounded,' not sent down to base hospitals, and of whom 77.2 per cent had returned to duty before the middle of November.

It would seem therefore that the total Allied losses were 489,334, 40,000 less than that of the Germans—perhaps 60,000 less. Now Mr. Churchill's figures for the British Somme casualties are an estimate, not an official return. He sees that the whole British loss on the Western Front from July 1 to November 18 was 463,000, and then deducts an arbitrary 53,000 for five months' losses on the whole front outside the Somme area. Thus he brings the Somme figures to 410,000, instead of the 342,667 quoted above. But the real casualty list on the rest of the front from July to November was not 53,000, but over 100,000. It is often forgotten how heavy was the day by day wastage in five months on a front of 100 miles, on which there was not only the normal loss which occurred all along the line at all times, but several sharp snatches of fighting on a considerable scale in front of Armentières, La Bassée, and Lens. For a period of 'stabilisation,' as it was grimly called, the normal British wastage was never so low as the 10,000 casualties per month which Mr. Churchill allows, and by which he obtains his 53,000 for losses not suffered on the Somme. One division lost 1700 men in a month, holding the sector by the Hohenzollern Redoubt.

Mr. Churchill has printed on pages 187–192 of the *World Crisis* an estimate of casualties made by himself at the time of the Somme battle, which he communicated to the Cabinet in August, during the second phase of the operations. It was intended to prove—what he still apparently maintains—that the British losses were twice and thrice those of the enemy. But unfortunately all the German data in it are inaccurate. He disputes, for example, the statement that there had been thirty German divisions in action on the Somme by August 1, and will not allow for more than eighteen. To summarise his argument, he holds that statements that the Germans had brought up thirty divisions should be distrusted. Where could they have come from? The fact that units belonging to thirty separate divisions had been identified by contact, if true, was no proof. It might well have been that individual regiments, or battalions which were 'resting,' had been scraped up from different fronts to meet the local emergency. But this might not mean that more than the equivalent of six or seven complete divisions had been concentrated. If this were so, the Allies might not have been fighting more than fourteen or fifteen divisions, if so many.

Now it is quite true that at the time there were two mixed and heterogeneous 'groups' or very large divisions composed of units drawn in from various quarters in the German line—one counting as many as thirteen battalions under a General Liebert was fighting the French at the south end of the Allied line. But not counting Liebert's or Franke's 'groups,' thirty-six complete divisional units had been engaged on the Somme by August 1 and forty-five by August 31.[1] As fast as a division

[1] Details can be verified from the tables at the end of this chapter.

was used up and withdrawn it was replaced by another. So arguments based by Mr. Churchill on a theory that a small number of divisions were engaged, and that average divisional losses need not have been very high, were incorrect. The Germans were drafting in reserves from all quarters to replace tired and decimated divisions, just as we were doing ourselves. By the end of November, as the table appended to this chapter clearly demonstrates, ninety-four divisions in all had taken their turn, of which some thirty-eight had been given a double visit to the front line, with a long rest at the rear in the interval. The total may be made up to ninety-seven divisions if we add the two improvised 'groups' of July, and two provisional brigades under Generals Osten and Scholz which appeared and were dissolved again in August. It is worth noting that all the best German troops on the West Front were turned in sooner or later on the Somme. Of the six Guard divisions, into which the original Guard Corps and Guard Reserve Corps had been redistributed, every one had taken its turn—they counted 33,000 casualties between them before November had come to an end. And every old 'active army' division in the West had been thrown in, except a few which had been so nearly exterminated at Verdun, during the spring or early summer, that they had to be built up anew and trained for months before they could be used for work of a responsible kind.

For the stress on the Somme was far harder than anything experienced at Verdun—the heaviest German casualties of the most critical month on that front were less than half of those reported in either of the months of August, October, or November in the Somme battle area. And at Verdun failure was merely failure—on the Somme it would have meant complete ruin. Hence the reckless fashion in which troops were heaped upon that rather narrow front ; and the perpetual and costly counter-attacks, which were made to regain each furlong of trench that the Allies succeeded in overrunning. The whole event of the war depended, for the Germans, in keeping their line in front of Bapaume unbroken—it was bent back, not pierced, and this they considered worth the 500,000 casualties suffered. But the losses were heartbreaking, and the general effect on their *moral* depressing. Ruin escaped is not the same thing as victory.

From the two latest German commentaries of value which I have seen, I extract the following frank confessions :

> ' The loss of ground was of no strategic importance. But the importance of the course of the fighting must not be measured by this. The great losses in men, the heavy expenditure of material, ate only too deep into the strength of the German army. The mighty material superiority of the enemy did not fail to have its psychological effect on the German soldier. The enemy commanders may put this down on the credit side, as a profit of their attrition-purpose. . . . The Old Army disappeared in the long-drawn battle.'
>
> ' Germany had been brought near to certain

collapse (sicheren untergang) by the Somme battle in 1916, as by the Flanders battle in 1917.'

I hold therefore that no Englishman should consider the Somme battle an error or a fruitless expenditure of blood, as Mr. Churchill still seems to maintain. The main thing to remember is that if the great attack had not been delivered our Allies could not have held out much longer at Verdun. This was avowed by their statesmen and generals to the British Cabinet and the British Headquarters, when they pleaded, not for a mere diversion, but for an assault that should draw all German reserves away to the west, and make it impossible for the pressure on Verdun to be maintained. Such an assault was made—it saved Verdun : it dented in the German Front in a way that struck terror to the enemy. It enabled the French in November and December to wipe out all that the Germans had gained before Verdun at tremendous cost. It brought their *moral* down to a lower level than it had reached since the battles of the Marne, now two years in the past. It cost the Germans 500,000 of their best troops : it effectively prevented any further offensive on their part for a very long time. Indeed, they showed their appreciation of the fact, by drawing back a long section of their front to a defensive position, far to the rear, before the fighting of the next spring began. Wherefore, though the German line was not actually broken, nor a decisive victory achieved, I cannot agree with those who look upon the Somme battles as a tale of unrelieved gloom and wasted effort.

GERMAN INFANTRY CASUALTIES

As given by the "Verlustliste" down to December, 1, 1916.

N.B.—A very few early casualty-reports given in late numbers of July are added to the August totals. The date of publication of losses grew steadily later as the months wore on. The word "incomplete" in the November column means that only part of the unit in question had published its losses when the printing ceased.

Name of Unit.	Present on the Somme Front between the subjoined dates.	August reports.	September reports.	October reports.	November reports.	Total.
Guard Corps—						
1st Guard Division	(1) From Aug. 15–Sept. 5	}	7,237	3,960	283 (incomplete)	11,480
2nd Guard Division	(2) From Oct. 20–Nov. 30	}	256	Sent to Russia in Sept.	—	5,010
3rd Guard Division	Early July only	4,754				
4th Guard Division	(1) July 25–Aug. 19. (2) Mid-Sept. (3) Nov. 6–25	} 1,680	2,985	671	962 (incomplete)	6,298
1st Guard Reserve Division	(1) July 20–Aug. 19. (2) Mid-Sept.	1,294	1,391	2,220	229	5,134
2nd Guard Reserve Division	July 1–Sept. 20	3,152	777	1,709	344	5,982
III Corps—						
5th Division	July only	4,472	79	—	—	4,551
6th Division	Oct. 8–29	—	—	8	3,235	3,243
IV Corps—						
7th Division	(1) July 4–28. (2) Sept. 17–Oct. 2	} 8,964	1,416	4,548	2,219	17,147
8th Division	(1) July 5–25. (2) Sept. 18–Oct. 1	}				
7th Reserve Division	Sept. 23–Oct. 10	—	—	—	2,527 (incomplete)	2,527
V Reserve Corps—						
9th Reserve Division	Sept. 25–Oct. 18	}	—	804	2,811 (incomplete ?)	3,615
10th Reserve Division	Oct. 5–15	}				

Unit	Dates at front					Total
VI Corps— 11th Division 12th Division	(1) July 1-20. (2) Sept. 5-Oct. 10 (1) July 1-14. (2) July 30-Aug. 9 (3) Oct. 25-Nov. 19	10,283	1,873	2,799	1,737 (incomplete ?)	16,692
VI Reserve Corps— 11th Reserve Division 12th Reserve Division	(1) July 1-20. (2) Oct. 1-31 (1) July 1-14. (2) Sept. 25-Nov. 5	10,825	820	762	2,404 (incomplete ?)	14,811
VII Corps— 13th Division	Sept. 12-19	—	—	2,490	740	3,230
VIII Corps— 15th Division 16th Division	(1) July 20-Aug. 10. (2) Oct.10-30 (1) July 20-Sept. 30. (2) Oct. 9-29	1,880	4,376	2,702	3,296 (sent to Russia in Nov.)	12,254
VIII Reserve Corps— 15th Reserve Division 16th Reserve Division	Both lent units to Liebert in July; whole of both divisions at front Oct. 15-Nov. 15	4,524	1,621	3,867	472 (incomplete)	10,484
IX Corps— 17th Division 18th Division	(1) July 9-25. (2) Aug. 20-Sept. 15 July 15-Sept. 20	7,031	3,804	5,982	472	17,289
IX Reserve Corps— 17th Reserve Division 18th Reserve Division	(1) July 25-Aug. 14. (2) Sept. 21-Oct. 9 (1) July 28-Aug. 14. (2) Oct. 6-20	7,192	4,196	2,703	2,023	16,114
19th Reserve Division	Oct. 10-26 only	—	—	—	1,097 (incomplete)	1,097
22nd Reserve Division	July 1-10 only	3,339	255	—	—	3,594
XI Corps— 38th Division	Oct. 12-Nov. 12	—	—	—	960 (incomplete)	960
XII Corps— 23rd Division 32nd Division	Lent units to Franke in July. Whole division Sept. 15-Oct. 25 Lent units to Franke in July. Whole division in Nov.	1,825	3,816	5,111	2,667	13,419

Name of Unit.	Present on the Somme Front between the subjoined dates.	August reports.	September reports.	October reports.	November reports.	Total.
XII Reserve Corps—						
23rd Reserve Division 24th Reserve Division	(1) July 20-Aug. 12. (2) Oct. 15-Nov. 20 (1) July 10-26. (2) Nov. 15-Dec. 12	9,270	2,947	2,227	1,315 (incomplete)	15,759
XIII Corps—						
26th Division 27th Division	(1) Late July-Aug. 25. (2) Mid-Nov. (1) Aug. 1-25. (2) Mid-Nov.	770	2,768	5,447	1,115 (incomplete)	10,100
XIV Corps—						
28th Division 29th Division	July 20-Oct. 5 Sept. 20-Nov. 25	1,666	526	1,827	1,267 (incomplete)	5,286
XIV Reserve Corps—						
26th Reserve Division 28th Reserve Division	(1) July 1-13. (2) Mid-Oct. (1) July 1-13. (2) Mid-Oct.	9,618	1,867	2,142	2,861	16,488
XV Corps—						
30th Division	Oct. 1-Nov. 20	—	—	500	1,340 (incomplete)	1,840
39th Division	Oct. 27-Nov. 11	—	—	—	308 (incomplete)	308
XVII Corps—						
35th Division 36th Division	July 1-Sept. 5 July 1-Nov. 25, intermittently	4,520	320	3,267	760	8,867
XVIII Corps—						
21st Division	(1) Sept. 12-Oct. 1. (2) Late Nov.	—	—	4,519	2,484	7,003
25th Division	(1) Sept. 21-Oct. 1. (2) Late Nov.	—	—	3,267	760 (incomplete)	4,027
XIX Corps—						
24th Division 40th Division	(1) Aug. 8-20. (2) Sept. 20-Nov. 10 (1) Aug. 8-20. (2) Oct. 15-Nov. 11	650	8,287	898	3,026	[12,861
XXII Reserve Corps—						
44th Reserve Division	(1) July 3-10. (2) Oct. 9-30	3,710	144	846	3,925	8,625

Division	Date					
XXIII Reserve Corps—						
45th Reserve Division / 46th Reserve Division	(1) Sept. 9-25. (2) Oct. 20-25 / (1) Sept. 8-Oct. 9. (2) Oct. 20-25	—	—	6,780	2,010	8,790
XXV Reserve Corps—						
50th Reserve Division	(1) Sept. 20-28. (2) Nov. 10-30	—	—	180	860 (incomplete)	1,040
XXVI Reserve Corps—						
51st Reserve Division / 52nd Reserve Division	Sept. 15-Oct. 1 / Sept. 15-Oct. 1	—	—	3,095	3,684 (incomplete)	6,779
XXVII Reserve Corps—						
53rd Reserve Division / 54th Reserve Division	Sept. 1-15 / Sept. 1-18	2,020	2,289	6,856	2,809	11,954
52nd Reconstituted Division	Sept.-Nov.	—	709	592	2,114	5,445
56th Reconstituted Division	Aug. 24-Sept. 9	—	2,114	1,447	81	3,642
58th Reconstituted Division	Sept. 10-Nov. 5, intermittently	—	—	906	1,214 (incomplete)	2,120
103rd Reconstituted Division	Oct. 8-Nov. 10	—	—	—	452 (incomplete)	452
111th Reconstituted Division	(1) July 1-20. (2) Aug. 26-Sept. 6. / (3) Oct. 25-Nov. 20	?	940	1,890	500 (incomplete)	3,330
113th Reconstituted Division	(1) July 1-15. (2) Oct. 1-15	690	—	219	1,869	2,778
117th Reconstituted Division	July 20-Aug. 15	1,996	1,559	Sent to Russia	—	3,555
121st Reconstituted Division	July 1-4 only	5,625	653	Sent to Russia	—	6,278
123rd Reconstituted Division	July 5-22	3,905	1,472	Sent to Russia	—	4,398
183rd Division	(1) July 1-24. (2) Oct. 1-20	3,498	71	363	1,500	6,833
185th Division	(1) July 1-18. (2) Sept. 7-Oct. 25. / (3) Nov. 10-Dec. 9	3,879	—	1,070	28	5,048
206th Division	Oct. 20-Nov. 15	—	—	—	497 (incomplete)	497
208th Division	Nov. 18-Dec. 12	—	—	—	710 (incomplete)	710
211th Division	Oct. 14-Nov. 6	—	—	—	1,774 (incomplete)	1,774

Name of Unit.	Present on the Somme Front between the subjoined dates.	August reports.	September reports.	October reports.	November reports.	Total.
212th Division	(1) Sept. 15–Oct. 5. (2) Oct. 25–Nov. 25	—	—	2,431	1,041 (incomplete)	3,472
213th Division	(1) Sept. 15–Oct. 15	—	—	3,341	120 (incomplete)	3,461
214th Division	Sept. 14–28 only	—	—	986	2,705 (incomplete)	3,691
221st Division	Oct. 21–Dec. 1	—	—	—	616 (incomplete)	616
222nd Division	Nov. 5–Dec. 1	—	—	—	298 (incomplete)	298
223rd Division	Nov. 9–21	—	—	—	No reports	—
243rd Division	Oct. 3–Nov. 16	—	—	960	No reports	960
4th Ersatz Division	Sept. 27–Oct. 14	—	—	124	3,479	3,603
5th Ersatz Division	Oct. 19–Nov. 20	—	—	—	No reports	—
10th Ersatz Division	Sept. 10–25	—	—	3,526	52	3,578
Marine Division	Sept. 20–Nov. 15	—	—	—	2,910 (incomplete)	2,910
I Bavarian Corps— 1st Bavarian Division	Oct. 13–end of Nov.	—	—	212	1,781 (incomplete)	1,993
2nd Bavarian Division	Late Oct.–late Nov.					
II Bavarian Corps— 3rd Bavarian Division	Aug. 25–Sept. 27	—	—	5,338	5,091	10,429
4th Bavarian Division	Aug. 25–Sept. 27					
III Bavarian Corps— 5th Bavarian Division	Sept. 7–20	—	—	3,788	6,534	10,322
6th Bavarian Division	Sept. 7–27					
Bavarian Reserve Corps— 1st Bavarian Reserve Div.	(1) Aug. 8–13. (2) Aug. 25–Sept. 10	293	2,650	6,023	—	8,966
5th Bavarian Reserve Div.	Aug. 8–Sept. 10					
6th Bavarian Reserve Div.	Sept. 27–Oct. 13	—	—	545	3,707	4,252

Division	Period			Sent to Roumania	Sent to Russia	Total
8th Bavarian Reserve Div.	July 20–Aug. 15	1,492	4,247	—	—	5,739
10th Bavarian Division	July 1–20 only	3,215	2,429	—	—	5,644
14th Bavarian Division	Nov. 15–Dec. 15	—	—	—	700 (incomplete)	700
Bavarian Ersatz Division	Oct. 25–Nov. 25	—	—	—	No returns	—
Total		128,042	71,387	115,948	96,775	412,152
Add returns not accounted for above from Liebert's and Franke's provisional divisions, Scholz's and Osten's provisional brigades (some of all these are accounted for under their proper corps) and from other fractional units.	Liebert's and Franke's division operated in July. Scholz's and Osten's brigades in August. The other fractional units operated at various times in very varying force.	5,638	2,263	1,760	3,143	12,804
		133,680	73,650	117,708	99,918	424,956

CHAPTER III

MR. CHURCHILL'S OPINIONS
SOME OTHER POINTS OF VIEW

By MAJOR-GENERAL SIR W. D. BIRD

K.B.E., C.B., C.M.G., D.S.O.

(Published in *The Army Quarterly*, July 1927.)

THE substance of much of Mr. Churchill's latest book, so far as military operations are concerned, may not unfairly be summed up in the words : ' It is the folly of the world constantly which confounds its wisdom.' The shortcomings, as he believes, of the higher commands are laid bare with unsparing hands, and although praise at time is not withheld from some of the leaders, the French General Michel is one of the few who receives unqualified approval.

In the summer of 1910 General Michel became Vice-President of the *Conseil supérieur de la guerre,* and soon afterwards he worked out a plan of concentration and operations for the French Army in case of war with the Germans, which was based on a new method of using the reserve formations ; that is, the formations composed of men between about twenty-five and thirty-five years of age who had completed their term of service in the active army.

According to Mr. Churchill, General Michel affirmed that :

' the German General Staff would use immediately not only their twenty-one active corps, but, in addition, the greater part of the twenty-one reserve corps which it was known they intended to form on general mobilization. France therefore should be prepared to meet an immense turning movement through Belgium and a hostile army which would comprise *at the outset* the greater part of forty-two army corps. To confront this invasion he proposed that the French should organise and use a large proportion of their own reserves from the very beginning. For this purpose he desired to create a reserve formation at the side of each active formation, and to make both units take the field together under the officer commanding the active unit. By this means the strength of the French Army would be raised from 1,300,000 to 2,000,000, and the German Army would be confronted with at least equal numbers. . . . These forces General Michel next proceeded to distribute. He proposed to place his greatest mass, nearly 500,000 strong, between Lille and Avesnes to counter the main strength of the German turning movement (see Sketch 1). He placed his second mass, 300,000, on the right of the first between Hirson and Rethel ; he assigned 220,000 for the garrison of Paris, which was also to act as general reserve. His remaining troops were disposed along the Eastern frontier. Such was the plan of the leading soldier of France. These ideas ran directly counter to the main stream of French military thought. The General Staff did not believe that Germany would make a turning movement through Belgium, certainly not through northern Belgium. They did not believe that the Germans would use their reserve formations in the opening battles. They did not believe that reserve formations could possibly be made capable of taking part in the struggle until after a prolonged period of training. They held, on the contrary, that the Germans, using only their active army, would attack with extreme rapidity and must be met and forestalled by a French counter-thrust across the Eastern frontier. . . . It may be that his (Michel's) personality and temperament were not equal to the profound and penetrating justice of his ideas. . . . An overwhelming combination was formed against him by his colleagues on the Council of War. . . . The Vice-President found himself alone ; almost every other general declared his direct disagreement.'

It may be inferred from the above that, according to the information on which Mr. Churchill relies, the early employment of reserve formations was discountenanced by the French military experts. This, however, was not the case, for even under Plan XVI for the defence of France against Germany, which was made in 1908, reserve formations were placed among the troops of the general reserve. The proposal that actually was rejected by the members of the *Conseil supérieur de la guerre* was that of using at once men of the reserve formations in the front line. But, apart from this, General Michel's organisation was clumsy, namely, a demi-brigade of three active and three reserve battalions, a brigade of twelve battalions and a company of engineers, and a division of twenty-four battalions, twenty batteries, and four companies of engineers. Since the basis of General Michel's plan had not been approved, the plan itself, according to the account compiled under the direction of the French War Office—*Les Armées françaises dans la Grande Guerre*—was not discussed.

Mr. Churchill seems to think that General Michel intended to stand on the defensive and to wait for the Germans; whereas he wrote in his plan:

'*La masse offensive comprendrait donc :* (1) *Pour opérer en Belgique entre la mer et la ligne Sambre et Meuse . . .* 490,000 *hommes.* (2) *Pour opérer à la droite des premiers . . .* 280,000 . . . *auxquels pourrait s'ajouter les* 220,000 *autour de la capitale. . . . La defense de la frontière entre Montmédy et Belfort, constitue par les garnisons territoriales des places fortes et les* 300,000 *hommes de troupes actives . . . pourrait être renforcée ultièrement par . . . d'environ* 200,000 *hommes . . . nous donnerait également une attitude offensive en Lorraine et en Alsace.*'

When, in 1905, the German Count von Schlieffen drew up his final plan of campaign in case of war between Germany and Austria on one side, and France and Russia, with the assistance of Great Britain, on the other, he was convinced that a decisive defeat could more easily be inflicted on the French than on the Russians; that whatever action was taken by the Germans, that is, whether they respected or violated Belgium, Great Britain would certainly join the French if they were involved in a war with the Germans; that the main French Army would be placed in the area to the south of Mezières; and that it would be very difficult, if not impossible, rapidly to break through the fortified lines of the French, which ran, with only one gap, from Verdun to Belfort. He also believed that, if these fortifications were avoided by moving the bulk of the German Army through Belgium, the Germans, by making a complete wheel to the left, with the German fortified areas of Metz and Strasburg as pivot, could envelop, defeat, and drive the forces of the French south-eastward until they were finally hustled against their own fortresses and the Swiss frontier. The skeleton of this plan was adopted by Schlieffen's successor as Chief of the General Staff, General von Moltke; but, while in Schlieffen's plan a very powerful right wing was to continue its wide wheel whatever action was taken by the French, Moltke intended at once to close in on and try to envelop the French armies if they advanced into Lorraine from their lines of fortresses. And Moltke estimated, with fair accuracy, that these armies would be concentrated in five groups near La Fère, Rethel, Nancy, Épinal, and Vesoul with, a reserve between Châlons and Chaumont.

The information actually possessed by both Schlieffen and Moltke of the dispositions that might be made by the French was not without influence on the plans of the Germans. It is at least not improbable therefore that, when information had been obtained of so radical a change as that proposed by General Michel—and, according to the experience of both French and Germans, it is impossible to keep quite secret the arrangements for moving by rail and concentrating large masses of troops—equally drastic alterations would have been made in the dispositions of the Germans. For instance, one of the variations of Schlieffen's plan might have been adopted, under which if the French invaded Belgium they were both to be stopped on the line Namur–Liège, and their right centre attacked by forces advancing from the area Metz–Thionville–Trèves. Or the Germans might have decided on the plan of invading France through Switzerland, which is fully explained by General Berthaut in *L'Erreur de* 1914, relying on the guarantees given by the Powers as to the neutrality of Belgium to protect the munition factories of the Ruhr.

To the professional military mind the political objections to such a concentration as that proposed by General Michel seem, however, to be even stronger. It is surely probable that, as soon as they found out the dispositions to be made by the French, the Germans would have suggested to the Belgians and British that it was evident that France was determined to drag them into war by challenging, even compelling, Germany to invade Belgium in defence of the vital area of the Ruhr; and the effect of such revelations on opinion in Belgium and Great Britain might have been far-reaching. This was realized by the French, who naturally wished above everything to avoid such accusations; and in consequence, as stated by M. Reinach:

> '*La concentration telle que l'a prévue l'état-major français part de cette donnée que la politique*

*et la diplomatie, et l'honneur, ont imposée à la
stratégie : Respecter la neutralité du terrain belge
n'y pénétrer que si les Allemands y entrent. En
outre cette volonté française d'observer les traités
internationaux qui portent la signature de la France,
il faut qu'elle soit évidente, qu'elle apparaisse claire-
ment aux alliés éventuels et aux neutres. Le dis-
positif initial ne doit prêter à aucune ambiguïté.'*

After the rejection of General Michel's plan, the
appointment of Vice-President of the *Conseil
supérieur de la guerre* was abolished, and at the
same time General Joffre became *chef d'état-major
général*. Mr. Churchill has little to say in favour
of the plans and actions of this officer. On the
other hand, he deplores ' the immense miscalcula-
tions and almost fatal errors made by General Joffre
or in his name.' And we are also told that against
2,000,000 men who marched to invade France and
Belgium, General Joffre could only muster
1,300,000, of whom 600,000 were reservists :

' 1,200,000 additional French reservists responded
immediately to the national call, encumbering
the depôts, without equipment, without arms,
without cadres, without officers. In consequence,
the Germans outnumbered the French at the outbreak by *three to two* along the whole line of
battle. . . . At Charleroi they were *three to one*.'

Mr. Churchill says, in addition, that :

' In 1914, during four days from August 21
to 24 inclusive, 80 German divisions were engaged with 62 French, 4 British, 6 Belgian. The
four decisive days of the Marne, September 6

to 9 inclusive, involved approximately the same numbers.'

A rather different impression is obtained from the account issued by the French War Office and from the German official account, *Der Weltkrieg, Bearbeitet im Reichsarchiv*. It seems from the former that information, dated October 9, 1913, of the German plan of concentration fell into the hands of the French, and its analysis then put an end to any doubts that may have existed that German reserve corps would be mobilised and used in the same way as the active corps. The French estimated that 20 active corps, out of 25 that were available, each of 2 divisions, would be sent against France, as well as 10 reserve corps, each of 2 divisions, 8 cavalry divisions, and 8 reserve divisions ; that is, a total of 68 infantry divisions and 8 cavalry divisions. It was also inferred that the detraining of the active corps would be finished on the tenth day of mobilisation, that of the fighting troops of the reserve corps on the twelfth day, and that all these formations could move forward on the thirteenth day, the 8 reserve divisions following later. According to the German official account, the Germans in fact used on the Western Front up to the battle of the Aisne, 23 active corps, including the 2 divisions of the so-called Guard Reserve Corps (that is, 46 active divisions), 12 reserve corps and 2 reserve divisions (that is, 26 reserve divisions), and 10 cavalry divisions ; and of these 2 active divisions, 2 Guard Reserve divisions, and 1 cavalry division, were withdrawn for dispatch to East Prussia on August 26. On the other hand,

6½ divisions of *ersatz* were formed and had reached Lorraine and Alsace between August 15 and 18, and a Marine division was brought early in September to watch the Belgian forces in Antwerp. The Germans, therefore, had in the field a maximum of 78½ active, reserve, and *ersatz* divisions between August 18 and 26, including the IX Reserve Corps, which had been guarding the Kiel Canal.

Under Plan XVII (see Sketch 1), which was approved in 1913, the French intended to mobilise against Germany in round numbers 46 active divisions, nearly 1,000,000 men ; 25 reserve divisions, 450,000 men ; 10 cavalry divisions, 52,500 men ; army troops, 187,000 ; 12½ territorial divisions, 184,600 ; line of communication troops, 210,000 ; garrisons, 821,000 ; troops for depôts, 680,000 ; a total of 3,580,000. The active formations were to be ready to entrain between the third and ninth days of mobilisation, the reserve formations between the ninth and twelfth days, and the territorials between the fifth and fifteenth days. The peace establishment of the French Army in 1914 was about 726,000 ; between August 1 and 15, 1914, 1,710,000 reservists were called up, 1,100,000 territorials, 77,000 men for auxiliary services, and there were 71,000 volunteers—a total of 3,694,000 men. It is also stated in the French account that :

'*à partir du 2 août, les opérations de mobilization se sont déroulées méthodiquement conformément aux prévisions du plan XVII.*'

In Plan XVII, 46 active divisions and 14 reserve

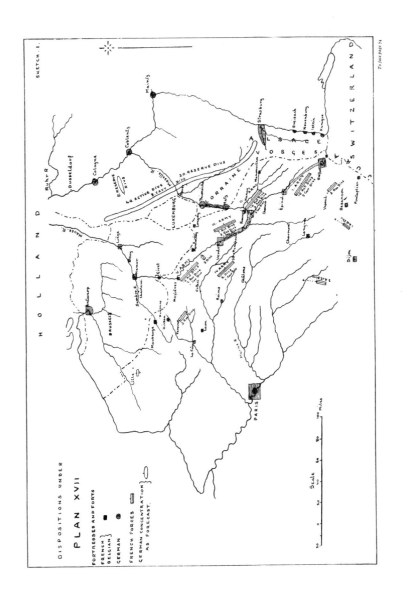

DISPOSITIONS UNDER

PLAN XVII

FORTRESSES AND FORTS

FRENCH
BELGIAN ▮

GERMAN ◉

FRENCH FORCES ▯

GERMAN CONCENTRATION } ◯
AS FORECAST.

Scale

20   0   20   40   60   80   100 Miles

divisions (the 1,300,000 men mentioned by Mr. Churchill) were to be placed in the first instance in the line of battle against the Germans; but the reserve divisions were only to be used for the occupation of positions, for investments, and for the defence of ground that was difficult to attack, and similar duties. Between August 21 and 23 the number of French infantry divisions actually in the field (see Sketch 2), and excluding such formations as the group of Alpine *chasseurs,* the 5th Colonial Brigade, and territorial divisions, had increased to 47 active divisions and 22 reserve divisions; there were 4 British infantry divisions, the 19th Infantry Brigade came up on the 24th, and 6 Belgian infantry divisions besides Belgian garrison troops in Antwerp and Namur; a total of 79 divisions. On the same dates, and excluding the 55th *Ersatz* Brigade, the *landwehr,* and siege artillery and engineers, there were 78 German active, reserve, and *ersatz* divisions on the Western Front, but 5 of these were be-sieging or were round Namur, and 3 were at or near Liège.

At Charleroi the French had on the field 13 infantry divisions, 3 being reserve divisions 2 of which were not engaged; the Germans had 14 infantry divisions, but troops to the strength of 1 division lost their way in the woods to the east of the Meuse, and were not in close action. On the other hand, the northern and north-eastern defences of Namur were carried during the night of August 22–23, and the Belgian field troops, the 4th Belgian Division, and 3 French battalions quitted the place on the 23rd (the rearguard was surrounded), although the last of the forts held out until the 26th. The French retreated on the 24th from the battlefield of Charleroi.

As regards the forces engaged at the battle of the Marne, leaving out *landwehr*, territorials, and odd brigades and groups, there were on the frontage from the Ourcq to the vicinity of St. Dié on the Meurthe, between September 6 and 9, 68 German infantry divisions (in addition, 5 German infantry divisions were in Belgium, and 2 were besieging Maubeuge, which fell on September 8); on the same front there were 7½ French infantry divisions and 5 British infantry divisions. On the frontage from the Ourcq to St. Mihiel—that is, excluding the troops in Lorraine and Alsace—there were 44 German infantry divisions, 51 French infantry divisions, 5 British infantry divisions. It is, of course, obvious that the number of men in the ranks and their *moral* are as important as the number of formations in the line, and Mr. Churchill states that the losses of the French had been far greater than those of the Germans. On the other hand, the French apparently had received drafts to replace a good many of their casualties, whereas apparently no drafts had reached the armies of the German centre and right; and, according to General Baumgarten-Crusius, the German divisions of the right and centre at the battle of the Marne had scarcely half of their establishment. It may, however, be supposed that, on account of their earlier successes, the *moral* of the German troops was higher than that of the French.

The doctrine, says Mr. Churchill, ' of the offen-

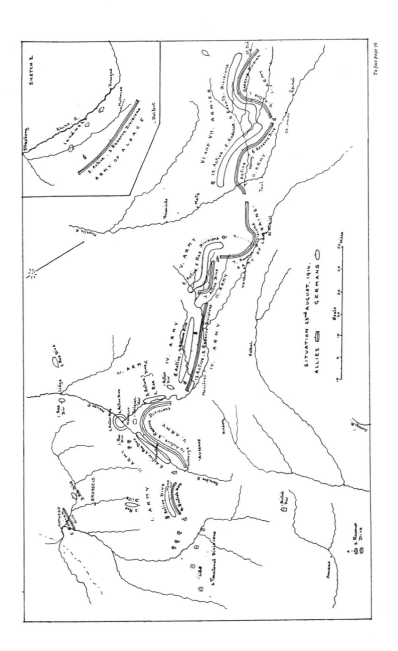

SKETCH 2.

ARMY OF ALSACE

2 Active 3 Reserve Divisions

Strasburg

Rhine R.

Landau

Mulhouse

Neu-Breisach

Belfort

VI AND VII ARMIES

12 Active 5 Reserve Divisions

6 Active 6 Reserve Divs.

VII ARMY

VI ARMY

II ARMY

Toul

Thionville

Metz

St. Dié

Château Salins

Épinal

Moselle R.

V. ARMY

6 Active 6 Res. Divisions

V. ARMY

III ARMY

VI ARMY

III ARMY

ARMY OF LORRAINE

7 Active 7 Reserve Divs.

Verdun

St. Mihiel

IV ARMY

6 Active 9 Divs.

Malmédy

11 Active 3 Reserve Divisions

IV. ARMY

III. ARMY

Liège

2 Reserve Divisions

1 Res. Div.

2 Active Divs.

Namur

3 Active Divs.

3 Res. Divs.

V. ARMY

10 Active 3 Res. Divisions

Maubeuge

Sambre R.

Avesnes

II. ARMY

6 Active Divs.

I. ARMY

BRUSSELS

BRUGES

ANTWERP

2016

2 Res. Div.

8 Active Divs.

British Divs.

British Divs.

Ostend

4 Territorial Divisions

SITUATION 23rd AUGUST, 1914.

ALLIES

GERMANS

Scale

0   10   20   30   40   50 Miles

= 1 Reserve Div.

= 1 Div.

sive raised to the height of a religious frenzy animated all ranks' of the French Army before the war. And it seems that this rage for attacking dated from the year 1911, when a Colonel de Grandmaison gave two lectures to the officers of the staff of the Army, which exercised a marked influence on new regulations then being drafted. In these lectures Grandmaison ridiculed the attempt to oppose ' *l'idée préconçue*,' the method the Germans were believed to favour, namely, that of deploying all their forces at once, and concentrating troops where it was intended to strike decisive blows, by ' *l'appréhension préconçue*.' And he advocated, therefore, that the French should, in the event of war, attack the Germans forthwith and before they could form their line of battle. And this plan, after all, is really founded on the point of view to which Mr. Churchill gave eloquent expression in the first volume of the series of works on the World Crisis, that :

' These same Germans were, of all enemies in the world, the most to be dreaded when pursuing their own plans ; the most easily disconcerted when forced to conform to the plans of their antagonist.'

So much impressed were the French authorities with the arguments of Colonel de Grandmaison that it was laid down, in regulations issued in 1913, that a commander can best assure his own liberty of action by imposing his will on the enemy through a strong offensive in accordance with a well-founded leading idea. The French proposed, then, to try and control events by attacking ; and it is evident that, to do this successfully, a nation must both hit very hard and keep on doing so. Such, right or wrong, appears to have been France's policy, and it was a policy under which there seemed also to be a good chance that her frontier would be kept inviolate ; a thing naturally to be desired, for no people wants the enemy to be brought to a stand-still even ' 30 to 50 kilometres ' inside the frontier, if he can be kept beyond it. For instance, when the 4th French Army was retiring on August 24, 1914, towards the Meuse, an old woman, whose outlook seems to have been typical of that of the population, stood at the door of her house, and pointing northwards called out to the troops : ' *Où allez-vous chasseurs ? La frontière n'est pas içi ! Elle est là-bas ! Lâches ! ' ' Elle écume comme une furie et ses invectives font baisser les fronts, détourner les têtes.*'

The dispositions that were made by General Joffre for the purpose of executing the military policy of his country are shown in Sketch 1. It was further contemplated under Plan XVII that the French should make two principal attacks : one by the 1st and 2nd Armies, which would advance into Lorraine from the area between the Vosges and the Moselle below Toul, their right being covered by a detachment operating in Alsace ; the other by the 5th Army in the district lying im-mediately north of a line between Verdun and Metz. The 3rd Army was to act as connecting link between the 2nd and 5th Armies, and the 4th Army was to be prepared to advance either on the left or on the right of the 3rd Army. The plan failed, but anyone who is inclined therefore to disapprove of it may, before condemning it altogether, not unprofitably try and draw up a better project. Remembering that it is national policy that is the foundation of a plan of campaign; vary the policy and a change of plan will inevitably ensue. Remembering, too, that when Plan XVII was made the actions of the Germans after their armies had reached the areas where they were to concentrate could only be guessed, the attitude that would be adopted by the Belgians was not known but their neutrality must be assumed, the policy of the Italians was doubtful, and the co-operation of the British by no means certain. And bearing in mind that political necessity obliged France to show to the whole world that she relied, and must continue to rely, on Germany's observance of the Prussian guarantee of the neutrality of Belgium, until there was definite proof that the Germans intended to incur the political and other disadvantages that would result from its violation.

Mr. Churchill laments the helplessness into which the art of war fell during the years from 1914 to 1918, the shortcomings of the higher commanders, and their inability to find the means of procuring a quick decision. But was land warfare in the late war really indecisive when compared with the majority of former wars? Did Thrasemene and Cannæ, or, to come to battles much nearer our own times, did Blenheim and Ramillies, and Minden, and the Alma, bring the nations nearer to a decision than the Somme and Arras? Apparently not. And it seems, then, that, in the case of war on land, at any rate, history shows that, whatever the size of armies and the efficiency of weapons, unless the first battles are really so decisive that the victor can rapidly clinch his success, the struggles between powerful rivals have more generally been long drawn out than brief. Even military geniuses like Hannibal and Marlborough could not, to quote Mr. Churchill's comment on the late war, quickly sever ' the chains which held the warring nations to their task ' during the Second Punic War and the long war of the Spanish Succession ; and the reason was that the conditions of the time hindered the first, and certainly prevented the second from doing so. It is possible, therefore, that it was not lack of 'military genius,' but similarity of circumstances that, ' leaving the fetters unbroken ' in the Great War, the fires of war were allowed to prey 'through fatal years upon the flesh of the captive nations.'

It may in broad generalisation be said that, in the opinion of the British General Staff, the British had no option but to concentrate in Northern France forces that would be fully adequate to safeguard the Channel ports and all the immense interests that depended on their security ; and that, in consequence, the troops that could be spared for other operations were strictly limited. And any one who wishes to learn what may be the consequences of incurring too great risks to the safety of vital interests, should refer to President Lincoln's measures during the Peninsular campaign of 1862 in North America. The General Staff also thought that ' Germany, with her central position and excellent railway system ' (see Sketch 3), as

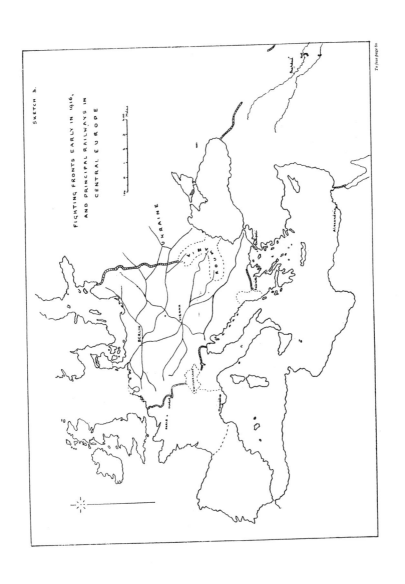

SKETCH 3.

FIGHTING FRONTS EARLY IN 1916,
AND PRINCIPAL RAILWAYS IN
CENTRAL EUROPE

Mr. Churchill describes it, could either meet with at least equal numbers, and after smaller expenditure of power and resources, large forces that were moved to theatres other than France; or could take advantage of their absence to defeat the British and French there. Further, for both military and political reasons, the British were constantly obliged to take the offensive in France so as to assist, or try to assist, their Allies; and for the reasons given above it would, in the view of the General Staff, have been disadvantageous to have made these attacks anywhere but in France.

Nearly a hundred years ago Clausewitz wrote that:

'The defensive is the stronger form of making war . . . it is very natural that the higher object (conquering) should be purchased by greater sacrifices. Whoever feels himself strong enough to make use of the weaker form (the offensive) has it in his power to aim at the greater object; whoever sets before himself the smaller object (preserving) can only do so in order to have the benefit of the stronger form . . . but . . . it follows of itself that we must only make use of it so long as our weakness compels us to do so, and that we must give up that form as soon as we feel strong enough to aim at a positive object.'

Mr. Churchill apparently is a follower of Clausewitz in believing that the defensive is the stronger form of making war, for he says:

'The question is . . . whether instead of seeking the offensive . . . both British and French ought not consistently on all occasions to have endeavoured to compel the enemy to attack ? '

It is, of course, not easy to compel the enemy to attack if it is not to his advantage to do so. As a rule, therefore, the best method of obliging the enemy to take the offensive is to invade his country and either to entrench there or to invest some locality the possession of which is of great value to the nation. Alternatively, a position may be seized, like that of Majuba Hill, which is so important to the enemy's army that there is no choice between attacking it or withdrawal elsewhere. Mr. Churchill suggests, however, that the enemy may be made to attack in another way :

' Suppose we have long selected and shrewdly weakened those portions where we can afford to give 20 or 30 kilometres of ground ; suppose we lure the enemy to attack there and make great bulges in a thin and yielding front, and then, just as he thinks himself pressing to final victory, strike with independent counter-offensive on the largest scale ... at the flanks of the moving, quivering line of battle. . . . Suppose that the British army sacrificed on the Somme, the finest we ever had, had been preserved, trained, and developed to its full strength till the summer of 1917, till perhaps 3000 tanks were ready, till an overwhelming artillery was prepared, till a scientific method of continuous advance had been devised, till the apparatus was complete, might not a decisive result have been achieved at one supreme stroke ? ' But he goes on to say that : ' From first to last it is contended that once the main armies were at deadlock in France the true strategy for both sides was to attack the weaker partners in the opposite combination with the utmost speed and ample force.'

It appears, then, that, if Mr. Churchill's strategy had been adopted, France would have been the ' main theatre, i.e. the theatre where the main forces are gathered,' but another area was to have been the ' decisive theatre, i.e. the theatre where the important decision can be obtained.' And Mr. Churchill's plan, as it seems, was to remain generally on the defensive on the Western Front, and to meet the objection : ' What of the Allies, what of Russia, what of Italy, would they have endured so long while France and Britain perfected their power ? ' by the reply that we could have held the Germans just as well in France by threatening an offensive as by making one ; and that direct aid could have been given to Russia through the destruction of Turkey, and to the Italians through the marshalling of the Balkan States against Austria.

The strategy that, in Mr. Churchill's opinion, should have been followed by the Germans resembles the strategy followed by the Elder Pitt in the Seven Years' War, when forces were sent to fight the French both in Germany, where they were strong, and in Canada, where they were weak. His strategy for the Western Powers is similar in principle to the strategy pursued by the British and their Allies, from 1704 onwards, during the War of the Spanish Succession. For they then both fought the French in Italy and on the Franco-Belgian border, despatched troops to assist the Portuguese against the Spaniards; and sent forces to north-eastern and eastern Spain for the purpose of helping the Catalonians and other Spaniards to support the claims of an Austrian Archduke, to the throne of Spain.

Mr. Churchill thinks that:

‘ the natural tendency of the naval and military point of view is to confuse the main and decisive theatres. Wherever the main part of the army or main part of the fleet is assembled always claims their partisanship.’

But when armed forces are separated, as in the Seven Years’ War and the War of the Spanish Succession, into two principal groups, the operations of each group are dependent on those of the other group, and neither can, as a rule, succeed without the help of the other. And if there is any overbalance of dependence, it is more often against the smaller group; for instance, Pitt said that America was conquered in Germany. Whichever group is the more independent, one thing is certain, that a group will not effect its purpose unless sufficiently powerful to do so. As the Confederate General Forrest is said to have replied when asked to explain the method in which his successes were gained in the Civil War in North America: ‘ I always gets there before him with the mostest men ’; nowadays we should say in superior force —a requisite that unfortunately is often overlooked. And does not this requisite imply that the operations of the group whose failure will be most disastrous to the general cause are the decisive ones ?

Before dealing with his policy in regard to the operations on the Western Front, it is necessary to consider Mr. Churchill's suggestion that, early in 1916, the Allies should, after the evacuation of the Gallipoli Peninsula, have gone back there and made a surprise attack on the Dardanelles, which were only being guarded by three Turkish divisions.

> ' A single mental conception,' he writes, ' would have transformed all the twenty allied divisions (then in the Eastern Mediterranean, at Salonika, in Egypt) sprawling in defensive or diversive functions into a vast army crouching . . . for a single convergent spring on to the Peninsula.'

It is an attractive plan, a tempting method of turning misfortunes to commodity. But it is said that imagination is a dangerous guide unless the practicability of its promptings is verified for the purpose of arriving at conclusions on which it is safe to act, and General Forrest's maxim must also be borne in mind. It is necessary, therefore, before agreeing that it would have been ' a thoroughly feasible scheme ' to consider first how the Bulgarian, and German, armies were to be held fast and prevented from anticipating the Allies at the Dardanelles ; and, secondly, even if there were ' immense quantities of shipping and small craft of all kinds . . . on the spot,' how all the preparations for the movement of the troops, their land transport, their food, their huge stores of munitions, could have been kept secret. And that immense quantities of shipping would have been required to move such forces quickly is evident from the calculation made in 1916 that a fleet of 279 ships would be needed to transport ten divisions from France to Salonika, a distance about twice that from Alexandria to Gallipoli, and that the movement could not be completed in less than five months. Also arrangements would have been needed for the protection of the shipping against attacks from submarines both during the voyage and when the disembarkation of the troops and their munitions was in progress ; and, in addition, the question must be faced, whether landings could be begun on open beaches, or in partly sheltered bays, during the stormy months of winter without unwarrantable risk.

After the Franco-German War of 1870–1871, when France was still weak, the French confided the fortification of the frontier facing Germany to General Sérè de Rivière, who built two great groups of fortresses there (see Sketch 1), leaving a mouse-trap at Charmes between the southern and central group, and another between the central system and the Belgian frontier and the small forts Longwy, Montmédy, etc., facing Belgian Luxemburg. And one of the reasons why the Germans invaded Belgium was because by doing so the mouse-traps were avoided. Mr. Churchill's plan for the fortification of the Allied front, the plan of long selecting and shrewdly weakening those portions where twenty or thirty kilometres of ground can be yielded without much risk, resembles that of General de Rivière ; but Mr. Churchill would have baited his mouse-traps by placing behind them the New British Armies and British Territorials, who would be completing their training, and by manufacturing numbers of tanks and big guns. The Germans, then, would be in the dilemma of being obliged to attack these strong positions before the arming and training of the troops had been completed ; or of making attacks elsewhere. And if the latter policy were adopted, the New Armies and the Territorials would be given the time in which to continue their instruction and armament ; unless the Allies were forced in their turn either to attack the positions of the Germans in France on account of the pressure that was being brought against the Russians and Italians, or to go directly to their assistance.

If both sides, after fortifying strongly the lines on the Western Front, had in 1916 (see Sketch 3) followed what Mr. Churchill thinks would have been their best plans, the British and French would have moved twenty divisions back to Gallipoli ; the Germans, instead of attacking Verdun, would, after taking measures to stop the Allies in France, have sent against Russia fifteen or twenty additional divisions, those with which the attack on Verdun was begun, ' animating the Austrian and Turkish armies ' ; and ' one half the effort, one quarter the sacrifice, lavished vainly in the attack on Verdun would have overcome the difficulty of the defective communications in the rich lands of the Ukraine.' The centre of gravity of the war would then have been shifted eastward ; but hardly to the advantage of the British and French, whose communications would have been the longer ones, and, owing to the operations of the crews of the German submarines, less secure than those of the Germans. And, in consequence, the Western Powers would have been forced to expend larger resources in maintaining troops in the eastern theatre in proportion to the resources used for the same purpose by the Germans.

Mr. Churchill draws a vivid picture of what would have happened if the British and French had pursued, in 1916, the policy that was actually followed by them, namely, that of attacks on the German lines in France, while the Germans attempted to break the blockade through the conquest of South Russia and its resources. And he claims that :

> ' The consequences of such a German policy must have paralysed all British war effort from her Indian Empire. In Egypt, in Mesopotamia, and in India whole armies of British and Indian troops would have been forced to stand idle in apprehension of impending invasion or revolt. ... At every stage her (Russia's) troops and those of her allies would have been dissipated in vain attempts to wall in the ever-spreading flood in the east, or would have been mown down in frantic assaults on the German trenches in France.'

It is evident that, if the Western Powers had not moved to the assistance of the Russians, the success of an offensive by the Germans against the Russians early in 1916 would have depended on the stability of the German front in France; the consequences of the failure of the Germans in 1918 prove this conclusively. Mr. Churchill thinks that the attacks the Allies would have made on it would have miscarried. But he also remarks that:

' It is certainly arguable that the French would have been wise to have played with the Germans at Verdun . . . while all the time the French would have been accumulating gigantic forces for an overwhelming blow on the Somme.'

If the Germans had made their attack on the Russians, not on Verdun, these gigantic French forces would have been available for an offensive on the German lines, and there were 41 British and Dominion divisions in France in February 1916, and 54 in June. Whether the strength of the Allies would have been sufficient to break the German front in France in 1916, held as it would apparently have been by about 100 divisions, that is, 120 less 20 sent to South Russia, before the Russian armies could have been utterly defeated, must remain a matter of opinion. The spring thaw would presumably have delayed the movements of the Germans in Russia; and, as regards the Western Front, it may be pointed out that, during the battle of the Somme, the Germans had ' roughly 120 divisions to the west of the Rhine,' and that Ludendorff says that there ' the situation gave cause for greater anxiety than I anticipated.'

' In all the British offensives,' writes Mr. Churchill, founding his conclusions on official figures, ' the British casualties were never less

than 3 to 2, and often nearly double the corresponding German losses . . . whereas while the
British suffered heavier losses in all offensives,
they exacted more than their own losses when
attacked by the Germans in 1918.'

The accuracy of these figures has been questioned,
but, in any case, it may be pointed out that it is
not a new phenomenon in war for the casualties of
the side that is attacking fortified or entrenched
positions to exceed those of the defenders. The
French garrison of Badajos in 1812 was 5000 strong,
and 4825 of the besieging Anglo-Portuguese army
were killed or wounded before the place was taken.
In 1864, during the Civil War in North America,
the Federals, according to Colonel Henderson, lost
27,000 men in attacking the positions of the
Confederates at Spotsylvania Court House and
Coldharbour, the Confederates 9700 men. At the
battles at Plevna in July, September, and December,
1877, the casualties of the Russians were 28,150,
those of the Turks 14,000 ; but when Plevna was
captured about 30,000 prisoners fell into the hands
of the Russians.

'You may prove anything by figures,' said
Carlyle, and in his book, *My War Memories, 1914-
1918*, General Ludendorff gives a reading different
from Mr. Churchill's of the figures of the casualties
of the Germans in the Great War. For he tells us
in regard to their experience that :

    ' The modern defensive battle is more costly
    than the attack, one reason more in favour of
    the latter . . . losses (in attack) consisted mainly

90

of slightly wounded men who came back. The prisoners we lost in the defence had to be struck off for good.'

If, as we are assured, the total casualties of the British were nearly 2,500,000, and those of the Germans only about 1,700,000, another conclusion which may be drawn from the figures is that when an 'untrained people,' to use Mr. Churchill's words, go to war with a nation in arms, the losses of the former are likely, for some time at any rate, to be much more numerous than those of the latter. In 1918, when the losses are said to have been more even, the Germans, according to Ludendorff, were no longer the troops of 1914, but 'only a kind of militia with much experience of war (trench fighting). The enemy was no better'; that is, the efficiency of the armies was then practically equal.

The Germans are said by Mr. Churchill to have been worn down in battle not 'by Joffre, Nivelle and Haig, but by Ludendorff' in the offensives in the spring and early summer of 1918. If so, the vicious system, which the Germans adopted, of using picked storm troops may largely have been to blame. For under this system the quick destruction of the 'finest and most audacious fighters' must inevitably result, and, in consequence, the rapid depression of general efficiency. Further, any failure by the storm troops must react unfavourably on the men of other formations, who will naturally ask how they can be expected to succeed in enterprises where chosen units have been baffled.

CHAPTER IV

JOFFRE, GALLIENI AND THE MARNE[1]
By MAJOR-GENERAL SIR F. MAURICE, K.C.M.G.

MUCH of the last two volumes of Mr. Winston Churchill's book on the Great War is, and I imagine was intended to be, highly controversial. Many of the points of controversy raised are not yet susceptible of historical treatment, for we still lack the authoritative information to enable us to form a considered judgment upon them. But in the early part of the first of these volumes Mr. Churchill returns to 1914, and for the period of the war up to the eve of the battle of the Marne we have now, at least as far as the conduct of the higher command on both sides is concerned, material as complete as is to be found for any period of military history. We have the British, French, and German official histories, and we have the personal accounts of almost every commander of armies on both sides, with the important exception of Marshal Joffre, who has maintained a resolute silence. Fortunately from the point of view of the historian that silence is not now a matter of much importance, for at the end of 1925 there was published the Second Part of the First Volume of the French Official History.[2] This deals .with the preliminaries of the battle of the Marne, and exhibits to us, in two large volumes of annexes, every relevant official military document.

[1] A lecture given in the University of London, May 10, 1927, and published in a slightly abbreviated form in the *Contemporary Review*, June 1927.
[2] *Les Armées Françaises dans la Grande Guerre.*

It is a cold narrative of fact, without comment and without description, but it and the documents attached enable us to read Joffre's mind from day to day, and at times even from hour to hour.

Now it is remarkable that these large and important volumes should have escaped the notice of Mr. Winston Churchill, more especially as he sets out to demolish Joffre's military reputation. ' This bull-headed, broad-shouldered, slow-thinking, phlegmatic, bucolic personage '[1] was, it appears, dragged reluctantly forward to the victory of the Marne by a man of energy, vision, and genius. Joffre, Mr. Churchill tells us,

> ' issued orders for a general retreat of the French armies, which contemplated their withdrawal, before resuming the offensive, not only behind the Marne but behind the Seine, and comprised the isolation or abandonment both of Paris and Verdun. . . . Joffre and the French Headquarters were withdrawing their armies with the avowed intention of turning on their pursuers and fighting a decisive battle at an early date. Exactly where and when they would fight they had not determined. All the armies were in constant contact, everything was in flux. But certainly they contemplated making their supreme effort at some moment when the five pursuing German armies were between the horns of Paris and Verdun.
> ' Galliéni's intervention decided this moment, and decided it gloriously. He it was who had

[1] Churchill, *The World Crisis, 1916–1918*, Vol. I, p. 22.

insisted on the defence of the capital when Joffre had advocated declaring it an open town. He inspired the Government to order Joffre to place a field army at his disposal for its defence. When the endless columns of the right-hand German army skirting Paris turned south-east, he decided instantly to strike at their exposed flank with his whole force. He set all his troops in motion towards the east; he convinced Joffre that the moment had come to strike; and he persuaded him that the flanking thrust should be made to the north rather than to the south of the Marne, as Joffre had proposed. Finally he struck his blow with all the sureness and spontaneity of military genius, and the blow heralded the battle that saved Europe.'[1]

Alas! most of this thrilling description is fiction! Let us turn to cold fact. General Galliéni was appointed Military Governor of Paris on August 26, 1914, and as such he took a very prominent part in the events leading up to the battle of the Marne. After the battle was over, and during the war, he wrote an account of his part in those events, which, we are told, he put away in a drawer without even re-reading it.[2] This document is an honest description of one part of a great whole, viewed from an angle. Galliéni was throughout the period he describes in, or in the immediate neighbourhood, of Paris. He was given by the Commander-in-Chief just sufficient information of events and of the latter's plans and

[1] Churchill, Vol. I, p. 25 et seq.
[2] *Mémoires du Général Galliéni. Défense de Paris*, p. 6.

intentions to enable him to play his part and no more. It is obvious that he knew little or nothing of the facts and influences which were determining Joffre's actions. If one may be critical of an account written in such circumstances, it may be said that it discloses a somewhat exaggerated view of the importance of the writer's actions, and it omits, probably owing to lapse of memory and haste in preparation, certain important facts and documents. After the war General Galliéni's family published this document under the title *Mémoires du Général Galliéni. Défense de Paris.* I am reasonably certain that had he lived General Galliéni would have revised it very considerably. As it is, it does him scant justice, but it is the way of pious relatives to injure by injudicious publications reputations which they hope to enhance.

The book was welcomed, and was the parent of numbers of subsidiary publications, all attacking Joffre. A scapegoat was required for the failure of Plan 17 and of the battles of the frontiers, and here was a handy stick to beat the victim, whom no blows could cause to break his silence. Mr. Churchill has accepted Galliéni and the assailants of Joffre as historical authorities of the first rank, and has neglected the French official history, which tells a very different story. To that story I will now turn.

On August 24, 1914, the breakdown of Plan 17 had become apparent. The French invasion of Alsace had failed, the battles of the frontiers had been lost, the Belgian Army was shut up in Antwerp, the full strength of the German turning movement through Belgium was disclosed, and the British Army had begun its retreat from Mons. In these circumstances of grave peril Joffre the next day issued General Instruction No. 2, which contained his new plan. The essential paragraph of this instruction runs : ' The projected offensive manœuvre being impossible of execution, future operations will be regulated with a view to the reconstruction on our left by the co-operation of the 4th and 5th Armies, of the British Army, and of new forces drawn from the region of the east, of a mass capable of resuming the offensive, while the other armies contain for the necessary time the effort of the enemy.' Here is the genesis of the battle of the Marne. For this plan promulgated on August 25 was brought to final and triumphant execution on September 9. For a ' slow-witted, phlegmatic, and bucolic personage ' it strikes me as remarkably prompt, bold, and broad of vision. It remained Joffre's plan for the next critical fortnight. Despite grave military friction and under the almost overwhelming burden of responsibility it is adhered to with sane resolution, being modified only in detail to meet changing circumstances from day to day. It envisages no piecemeal counterattack but a great offensive by four armies in combination. Its execution is at once begun and the new formation, Maunoury's 6th Army, later to be known to fame as the taxi-cab Army, begins to assemble on the Allied left about Amiens.

Incidentally I may mention that Mr. Churchill very much undervalues the skill with which Joffre withdrew his armies from the frontier and greatly exaggerates the losses which they suffered in the first battles. He says :

' Long swathes of red and blue corpses littered the stubble fields. The collision was general along the whole battle front and there was an universal recoil. In the mighty Battle of the Frontiers, the magnitude and terror of which is scarcely yet known to the British consciousness, more than 300,000 Frenchmen were killed, wounded, or made prisoners.'[1]

The Battle of the Frontiers Mr. Churchill elsewhere defines as the four days' battle from August 21 to 24. The French official history gives the total losses in the field armies, exclusive of officers, for the twenty-two days from August 10 to August 31 as 206,515 out of an effective strength of 1,600,000.[2] In the actual battles on the frontiers they were less than half Mr. Churchill's figure, and while there were on August 25 some French corps which had suffered severely, others had been but partially engaged. It was the fact that the Germans did not appreciate this and believed all the French armies to have been defeated decisively, which was one of the causes of their undoing.

On the same day on which Joffre issued his new plan, August 25, General Galliéni as Military Governor designate of Paris had an interview with M. Messimy, then Minister of War, at which the defenceless position of the capital was discussed,

[1] Churchill, Vol. I, p. 24.
[2] *Les Armées Françaises dans la Grande Guerre*, Tome I, Vol. II, p. 825. The figure 300,000 represents with approximate accuracy the entire French losses in Field Army, besieged garrisons and Territorial troops for the month of August.

and, on Galliéni declaring that at least three active corps would be needed for its defence, in addition to the Territorial and Fortress troops, the Minister telegraphed to Joffre: ' If our armies are not victorious and if they are compelled to retreat, an army of at least three active corps should be directed upon the entrenched camp of Paris to assure its defence.'[1] At that time the question of declaring Paris an open town or leaving it isolated had not arisen. The method of executing the Minister's order was left to Joffre, who was interposing his new 6th Army directly between von Kluck's right and Paris. The French Commander-in-Chief had, indeed, hoped to begin his counter-offensive on the Somme about the end of August, but the German pursuit was too rapid. On August 25 von Kluck caught up the 2nd British Corps and forced it to fight the next day at Le Câteau. Thereafter Sir John French retreated as rapidly as possible. He considered, and with justification, that he had been badly let down at Mons by General Lanrezac, the commander of the 5th French Army, who had retreated while we were still fighting at Mons without letting him know. Distrusting his French neighbours, and having a somewhat exaggerated view of the losses of his II Corps, Sir John thought primarily of bringing the little British Army into a position of greater safety. This upset Joffre's plans, and he moved the French President to telegraph on the matter to King George, with the result that the Prime Minister sent Kitchener to France. Meanwhile Joffre, in order to assist the

[1] *Les Armées Françaises*, Tome I, Vol. II, p. 581.

British Army in its exposed position, had ordered Lanrezac to attack von Bülow's 2nd German Army, which he did on August 29 in the battle of Guise. While the 5th French Army was attacking, the armies on its right and left were retreating, so that it became dangerously exposed, the more so as von Kluck had on August 30 decided, in response to an appeal from von Bülow, to swerve south-eastwards against Lanrezac's left flank. Lanrezac's right was simultaneously threatened by the advance against it of von Hausen's 3rd Army. The critical position of the 5th Army is shown by the sketch of the relative positions of the Allied and German Armies on the evening of August 30.

This 5th French Army was the largest of those designated for the counter-offensive, which could not therefore be made without it on the scale proposed. So from now on for several days Joffre's mind is mainly concentrated on disengaging his 5th Army, and on the date when it is disengaged depends the date of the counter-offensive. He endeavours to assist his 5th Army first, as we have seen, by trying to moderate the rate of the British retreat, and secondly by forming the left of his 4th Army, on Lanrezac's right, into a separate command and placing it under Foch. This detachment soon became the 9th French Army.

On September 1 Joffre issued a series of important orders. The most important of these is General Instruction No. 4, the salient passages of which are :

' Despite the success gained by our 3rd, 4th, and 5th Armies on the Meuse and at Guise, the enemy's outflanking movement directed against the left of our 5th Army and insufficiently checked by the British Army and our 6th Army makes it necessary to continue our retreat pivotting on our right.

'As soon as the 5th Army shall have escaped from the menace of envelopment, the 3rd, 4th, and 5th Armies together will resume the offensive. . . .

'The limit of the retreat, without any implication that this must be reached, may be taken to be . . . for the 5th Army behind the Seine.'[1]

On the same day Joffre ordered Maunoury's 6th Army to cover the northern and north-eastern fronts of Paris, and placed that army under the command of Galliéni. He had already ordered the 45th Algerian Division to Paris, and had directed Lanrezac to send his left corps, the XVIII, to the capital. But he found that the position of the 5th Army was too perilous to allow of this detachment, so he ordered Sarrail, who with the 3rd Army was covering Verdun, to send his IV Corps to Paris.[2] This corps began to entrain on September 2, and its leading divisions began to arrive on the 3rd. It was a part of one of the divisions of this corps which was sent forward by Galliéni in the taxis. Lastly, Joffre wired to the Minister of War also on September 1 :

'The Commander-in-Chief requests that the fortress of Paris should be placed under his orders . . . in order that, if opportunity arises, he may be

[1] *Les Armées Françaises*, Tome I, Vol. II, p. 532.
[2] *Les Armées Françaises*, Tome I, Vol. II, p. 529.

POSITIONS, EVENING, AUGUST 30, 1914

Le Câteau

Amiens

Beauvais

Breteuil

VI

Compiègne

R. Oise

R. Seine

PARIS

Melun

R. Seine

Meaux

R. Marne

Chateau Thierry

B.E.F.

Soissons

R. Aisne

Noyon

La Fère

Laon

Roye

St. Quentin

I von Kluck

II von Bülow

V

Reims

Rethel

Dt FOCH

III von Hausen

British
French
German

0   10   20   30   40   50 miles

To face page 100

able to combine the operations of the mobile garrison of the fortress with those of the field armies.'[1]

This message to the War Minister contains the first hint that has come from anyone of the manœuvre which eventually was carried out. It is in complete accord with the spirit of the order of August 25, but for the first time the possibility of a sortie from the defences of Paris is indicated. In fact, on September 1 Joffre had already received, mainly from the reports of British airmen, indications of von Kluck's swerve south-east. On the 2nd these indications were confirmed, but that evening some doubt set in. Part of the 1st German Army seemed to be advancing on Paris again. The reason for this was that some of von Kluck's cavalry and advanced guards in an incautious attempt to reach the flank of the 5th Army had bumped on September 1 into the British Army at Néry and Villers-Cotteret and had been roughly handled. In the hope of once more outflanking the British Army von Kluck had turned part of his army southwards, and it appeared to be again heading for Paris. The next day von Kluck, finding that we had eluded him, resumed his march south-eastwards, and of this Joffre had information on the evening of September 3. He then knew that Paris was in no immediate danger.

But, like the German armies, I have advanced too rapidly, and I must return to September 2. On that day Joffre issued a note to Galliéni and his army commanders in amplification of the general

[1] *Les Armées Françaises*, Annexe 1785.

instruction of September 1. This note, taken out of its context by certain critics, is the one which is produced as proof of Joffre's intention of abandoning Paris and Verdun, and, read superficially, it appears to indicate, particularly for the 3rd Army, the army of Verdun, a deeper retreat than does the General Instruction No. 4. But these critics have either wilfully or stupidly misread the note, and they have misled Mr. Churchill. Whereas Instruction No. 4 merely specified a general line for the limit of the retreat, with the saving clause which I have quoted, the note specifies as the general line for the termination of the retreat a number of railway stations farther back on main lines of railway, where the armies ' se recompléteront par les envois des dépôts.' Obviously depots of supplies and drafts must be fixed well behind the possible limit of withdrawal of the fighting troops, and in order that there may be no mistake, a reference is given in the note to the paragraph in the General Instruction No. 4, which contains the warning that the line indicated is a possible limit not necessarily to be reached. Joffre, looking at the position of his 5th Army, had calculated that it might possibly be necessary, in order to free it from the German armies, which menaced its front and flanks, and to give it room to turn round and form for attack, to withdraw that army behind the Seine, and his instruction to his army commanders was an indication of an eventuality which might arise, not an order to be obeyed literally. The tail of the 5th Army did, in fact, cross the Seine on September 5, so the calculation was not very far out. The note in amplification of the instruction is just such an one as a British Quarter-Master-General's Staff would draft as a supplement to a general staff order so that the armies might know where to receive supplies and drafts. It has nothing whatever to do with the abandonment of Paris or of Verdun.

The note of September 2 goes on to say that when the army had been sufficiently withdrawn the offensive will be assumed on the whole front, and concludes :

'the British Army will be asked to participate in this manœuvre. . . . Simultaneously the garrison of Paris will act in the direction of Meaux,'[1]

that is eastwards against von Kluck's flank. The plan grows in precision, and the armies are now told not only that the garrison of Paris will co-operate, but also the direction of its action. This note is received by Galliéni before any suggestion has come from him that the troops of Paris are to be employed otherwise than in defending the capital. For Galliéni is not yet aware, as Joffre is, of von Kluck's swerve to the south-east.

Meanwhile, on September 1 Sir John French had had a conference in Paris with Lord Kitchener and Mm. Viviani and Millerand, the French Prime and War Ministers, M. Millerand having taken M. Messimy's place. In arranging for the future action of the British Army Sir John had proposed to the War Minister that it should stand behind the Marne. M. Millerand had passed

---

[1] *Les Armées Françaises*, Annexe 1993.

this offer on to Joffre, who replied to him on September 2 :

'The present positions of the 5th Army do not allow of the realisation of the programme which Marshal French has indicated.'[1]

And in a letter to Sir John he amplifies this statement as follows :

'The present position of the 5th Army does not allow of that army assuring the British Army of effective support on its right. In view of what has happened in the past two hours I do not think it possible at the present time to envisage a combined manœuvre on the Marne with the whole of our forces.'[2]

What had happened during the past two hours was that a German force had penetrated to the communications of the 5th Army and had appeared to endanger the bridge over the Marne at Château-Thierry. Despite this, Joffre still sticks to his plan. He proposes to fight with the whole of his forces as soon as the 5th Army can take an effective part in the battle.

On the morning of September 3 Joffre sent to the Minister of War a memorandum reviewing the whole situation in these terms :

'The German right army has developed a wide turning movement against our left. We had hoped to meet this manœuvre by a powerful concentration in the neighbourhood of Amiens with the help of the British Army and the newly

[1] *Les Armées Françaises*, Tome I, Vol. II, p. 538.
[2] French, 1914, p. 97.

formed army under the orders of General Maunoury. The rapid retreat of the British Army, which took place before Maunoury's Army was ready to act effectively, has had deplorable consequences for the left flank of Lanrezac's Army, which on the afternoon of September 2 was to the north-east of Château-Thierry. The German cavalry crossing the Oise by a bridge which the English had not time to destroy was able to penetrate as far as our lines of communication, capturing a convoy, and it appeared on the evening of September 2 before Château-Thierry, where it attacked the bridges. To accept battle at the present time with any *one* of our armies would fatally involve the remainder, and the army of General Lanrezac would find itself in a position which the advance of the 1st German Army would make highly dangerous. The least check would bring with it the greatest risks of developing into an irremediable rout, in the course of which our other armies might be thrown back far from the entrenched camp of Paris and completely separated from the British forces.

'Our chance of success would be further diminished by the great fatigue of our troops, who have been fighting constantly, and who require drafts to fill the gaps in their ranks. I have consulted the army commanders, who are not favourable to an immediate general engagement. However, our position in the alliance imposes on us the duty of sticking it out, of gaining time, and of holding on our front the largest possible German forces. This we can only do if we avoid a decisive engagement in which we have not the greatest possible chances of success, while exhausting the enemy by attacks whenever favourable opportunity offers, as our armies have in fact been doing. The necessity of abandoning temporarily to the enemy a greater part of the national territory should not suffice to make us accept a general battle prematurely, if we had to fight under unfavourable conditions.

'These are the considerations which have influenced the decision I have taken, namely, to wait a few days before delivering battle while continuing the retreat so as to avoid a premature engagement: to draw at least two army corps from the armies of our right, while assigning to those armies a purely defensive rôle: to reinforce and rest our troops to the greatest possible extent: to prepare an early offensive in co-operation with the British Army and with the mobile troops of the garrison of Paris.'[1]

That night, September 3, Joffre having, as I have explained, now got definite information that von Kluck was not marching on Paris at all, wired to Galliéni, who had been just placed under his orders:

'Part of General Maunoury's Army should be pushed at once towards the east to menace the German right flank, in order that the left of the British Army may feel that it is supported on

[1] *Les Armées Françaises*, Tome I, Vol. II, p. 545.

this side. It would be well to inform Marshal French of this and to keep in constant relation with him.'[1]

So on September 1 Joffre had asked the War Minister to place Paris under his orders in order that he might combine the operations of its mobile garrison with those of his field armies; on the 2nd he had in his note to the commanders of armies and to Galliéni indicated Meaux as the direction of attack of the garrison of Paris; on the 3rd he had told Galliéni to move a part of Maunoury's army eastwards. Up to the evening of September 3 Galliéni was quite rightly occupied entirely with the defence of the capital, and all his communications to Joffre and the Minister of War are to the effect that he has not got sufficient troops to make Paris safe. On the 2nd he had wired to Joffre:

'Paris is absolutely unable to defend herself unless you give her at least three active corps.'

On the morning of September 3 he again telegraphed to Joffre:

'In default of orders to the contrary I will do my best to hold Paris as long as possible. But owing to the weakness of the defence, particularly on the north-eastern front, we are in danger, and on this point I insist, of seeing that front broken, if you cannot intervene at the proper time with a diversion.'[2]

[1] *Les Armées Françaises*, Tome I, Vol. II, p. 620.
[2] *Les Armées Françaises*, Annexe 2179.

At 6.30 p.m. on the evening of September 3 Galliéni, on returning to his headquarters from a visit of inspection of his troops and defensive works, received his first intimation of von Kluck's swerve to the south-east, which, as we know, had, with a partial and temporary interruption on September 2, been in progress since August 30, and of which Joffre was informed. He at once saw the opportunity which this movement offered him, but at first he thought the news too good to be true, and he required confirmation of it. That evening, therefore, having not yet received Joffre's instruction to push Maunoury eastwards, he issued an order to his 6th Army giving the information of the German movement south-eastwards and directing Maunoury to remain in his position :

' *Demain 4 Septembre la VIme Armée ne bougera pas. Elle renforcera son front par des travaux défensifs.*'[1]

At the same time he directed that cavalry and air reconnaissances should go out at dawn to confirm the information already obtained. At 9 o'clock on the morning of September 4, having received both this confirmation and Joffre's instructions that a part of Maunoury's Army is to be pushed eastwards, he issued a warning order to Maunoury to be ready to move in that direction, saying that he will give more precise instructions when he knows what the British Army will do. At the same time he made arrangements to reinforce Maunoury with all the mobile troops which Joffre had placed at his dis-

[1] *Les Armées Françaises*, Annexe 2187.

posal for that purpose. That done, he caused his Chief of the Staff, General Clergerie, to telephone to French G.H.Q. to say what had been done, and in a second telephonic communication Clergerie added that Maunoury was ready to move either to the north or to the south bank of the Marne. Clergerie expressed a preference for the north bank as being the quickest way of getting at the enemy.[1] Colonel Pont, the staff officer who replied, said that Joffre preferred the south bank as giving more time for the development of his full strength, and at noon Joffre confirmed this in a telegram to Galliéni saying that of the two proposals he preferred the south bank, the reason being that he was not yet assured that his 5th Army and the British Army were ready for battle. The sole foundation for the story that Galliéni himself on the telephone repeatedly urged Joffre to attack at once appears to be a reference by General Clergerie in his book *Le Rôle du Gouvernement militaire de Paris* to a further conversation which Galliéni is said to have had at 7 p.m. with Joffre. The French official historians have not been able to find any record of this conversation. Galliéni does not mention it. Clergerie's book is very inaccurate in other particulars and is grossly unfair to the British Expeditionary Force. His story cannot be accepted without confirmation. The positions on the evening of September 3rd, that is to say, those known to Joffre on the morning of September 4th, will explain his reply to Galliéni.

[1] *Les Armées Françaises*, Annexe 2354.

As will be seen, the right of the 5th Army was not, on the evening of September 3, across the Marne and its left had been driven back from Château-Thierry. Thus there was still danger that von Kluck would interpose some part at least of his 1st Army between the 5th Army and the British, and in any event there was no prospect of being able to make a combined attack on September 4 with the 5th, British, and 6th Armies. Joffre's immediate intention on the early morning of the 4th was still further to disengage his 5th Army, and as this would probably bring the German armies over the Marne in pursuit, he contemplated attacking them on the south rather than on the north bank of the Marne, and he so informed Galliéni.

After these communications with G.H.Q. Galliéni soon after 1 p.m. set out with Maunoury for British Headquarters. Sir John French was out, but the French generals found Sir A. Murray, the British Chief of the Staff, and arranged with him, subject to Sir John's approval, for a combined attack by Maunoury south of the Marne against von Kluck's left flank, while the British Army attacked the German left front. This was as far as Galliéni's proposal went. He did not envisage the co-operation of the 5th Army, which as we know was a main element in Joffre's plan, in fact as compared with the latter Galliéni's plan was a local effort to take advantage of a local opportunity. Having sent off a staff officer to French G.H.Q. with the scheme provisionally arranged with the British, Galliéni returned to Paris, arriving at his headquarters

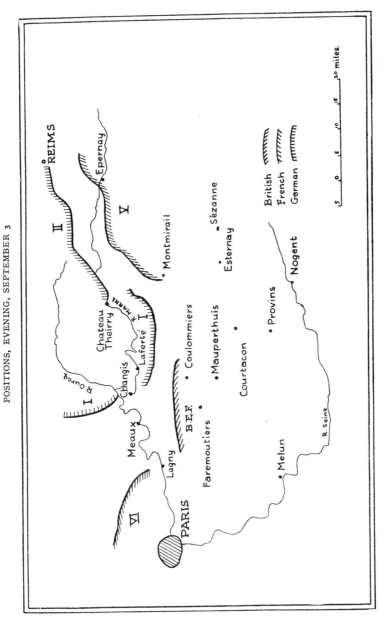

POSITIONS, EVENING, SEPTEMBER 3

PARIS

VI

Meaux

Lagny

Faremoutiers

B.E.F.

Melun

R. Seine

Changis

Laferté

Chateau Theirry

R. Ouroq

I

I

Coulommiers

Mauperthuis

Courtacon

Provins

Nogent

II

REIMS

Epernay

V

Montmirail

Esternay

Sézanne

R. Marne

British
French
German

5   0   5   10   15   20 miles.

To face page 110

about 7.30 p.m. Meanwhile decisive measures had been concerted elsewhere.

At 12.45 p.m. Joffre had telegraphed to the 5th Army, now commanded by Franchet d'Espérey, Lanrezac having been removed :

> ' The circumstances are such that it may be advantageous to deliver battle to-morrow or the day after with the whole of the 5th Army in concert with the British Army and the mobile garrison of Paris against the 1st and 2nd German Armies. Inform me immediately you can attack with prospect of success.'

When this message reached Franchet d'Espérey he was conferring with Sir Henry Wilson, at that time sub-Chief of the British General Staff, and the two together drew up a scheme of co-operation for the British Army and the French 5th and 6th Armies. That done, Franchet d'Espérey replied to Joffre :

> ' The 5th Army cannot be ready for battle till the 6th.
>
> ' On the 5th it will continue its retreat to the line Provins-Sézanne (that is a few miles north of the Seine).
>
> ' The British Army will change front facing east of the line Changis-Coulommiers on condition that it is supported on its left flank by the 6th Army, which should advance to the line of the Ourcq on September 5th.
>
> ' On September 6 the general direction of attack of the British Army and the 5th Army

should be Montmirail, that of the 6th Army
Château Thierry. The energetic co-operation
of the 9th Army is very desirable.'

This message Franchet d'Espérey followed with
another at 4.45 p.m. :

' The closest co-operation by the 6th Army on
the left bank of the Ourcq to the north-east of
Meaux on the morning of the 6th is essential.
It must be on the Ourcq to-morrow, Septem
ber 5th.'

It was on receipt of this message that Joffre,
having meanwhile heard from Foch that his 9th
Army was in a position to co-operate, turned to his
staff and said, ' Very well, gentlemen, we will fight
on the Marne,' and he then and there gave instructions for the preparation of the orders for the
battle of the Marne, which, issued that night, follow
almost textually the suggestions of d'Espérey and
Wilson.

The essential parts of the second and third
paragraphs of Joffre's order of September 4 run :

2. The dispositions to be realised by the evening
    of September 5 will be :
(a) All the available forces of the 6th Army to
    the north-east of Meaux ready to cross the
    Ourcq in the general direction of Château-
    Thierry. . . .
(b) The British Army established on the front
    Changis-Coulommiers facing east, ready to
    attack in the general direction of Mont-
    mirail. . . .

(c) The 5th Army, closing slightly to the left, will be established on the general front Courtacon-Esternay-Sézanne, ready to attack in a general south-north direction.

(d) The 9th Army (General Foch) will cover the right of the 5th Army, holding the southern exits of the marshes of St. Gond and sending a part of its forces to the plateau of Sézanne.

3. These various armies will be ready to take the offensive on the morning of September 6.

In his book, General Galliéni asserts that he issued the order for the advance of the 6th Army eastwards at 8.30 p.m. on September 4, that is two hours and a quarter before he received Joffre's telephone message, and he suggests that the hour of issue of Joffre's order was faked at French G.H.Q. in order to enable Joffre ' to claim the initiative in the eyes of history.'[1]

In this Galliéni's memory was clearly at fault; be it remembered that he never had time to revise his memoir, for the copy of the order in question, General Order No. 5, included amongst the documents of his book, is marked as having been issued at 10.30 a.m. on the 4th, which is clearly impossible,[2] while the French official history is positive that the order was not issued until the morning of the 5th. If any faking occurred it must have taken place in Galliéni's office, but it is more charitable to suppose that a *bona fide* mistake in marking was made due to the pressure of work in these critical

[1] *Mémoires du Général Galliéni*, p. 132.   [2] *Ibid.*, p. 225.

hours. The third paragraph of General Galliéni's Order No. 5 concludes :

' The 6th Army will be ready to attack on the morning of the 6th in liaison with the English Army, which will attack on the front Coulommiers-Changis.'

That is to say the order includes the plan for the British Army proposed by Wilson and Franchet d'Espérey, approved by Joffre, and communicated at 10.45 p.m. on the 4th to Galliéni. Now the plan which Galliéni and Maunoury had agreed upon with Murray was for the 6th Army to attack south of the Marne and for the British Army to be ready to advance on the front Mauperthuis-Faremoutiers, that is south and west of the line proposed by Wilson and d'Espérey, so as to allow room for the 6th Army to come in south of the Marne. Joffre's order of September 4 did not reach Sir John French until 3 a.m. on September 5, and meantime the British Army had made a short night march to the south in order to make room for the 6th Army in accordance with Galliéni's plan. No communication as to any change in this plan went on the evening of the 4th from British Headquarters to Galliéni, nor is there any record of any similar communication from Franchet d'Espérey to Galliéni. It is therefore clear that the news that the British Front was to be Coulommiers-Changis could only have come from Joffre, and, as Galliéni's order includes that news, it must have been subsequent to Joffre's message. In the event, owing to the late arrival of Joffre's orders and to the night march of September 4–5, the British Army was not able to occupy the line Coulommiers-Changis in the time indicated, but this did not affect the principle of Joffre's plan. As the following sketch shows, the four armies of the Allied left were on the evening of September 5 so placed as to be able to attack together, the situation Joffre had been endeavouring to bring about since August 25.

It was natural enough for Galliéni to suppose that it was his plan that had been accepted and his proposals to Joffre which had convinced the French Commander-in-Chief, for he was in complete ignorance of what had passed between Joffre and d'Espérey, and only knew that the 6th Army was to advance on the north bank of the Marne as he had through his staff officer suggested to G.H.Q. at 10 a.m. the morning of September 4.

Galliéni's part in the preparation of the plan of the battle of the Marne consisted in :

1. Passing to Joffre information of von Kluck's swerve to the south-east, which Joffre already possessed.
2. In preparing for a move by Maunoury eastwards in accordance with instructions which he had received from Joffre.
3. In reinforcing Maunoury with the mobile troops which Joffre had placed at his disposal for that purpose.

And possibly, not certainly,

4. Being the cause through his telephone messages on the morning of the 4th of Joffre

sending his telegram of 12.45 p.m. to d'Espérey, which called forth the proposals for
the battle which actually became effective.

I say that this is possible, but not certain, for we
have as yet no precise information as to what
caused Joffre to send that message. It was a
natural one for him to have sent in view of the information of von Kluck's movements, in view of
the fact that he learned on the forenoon of the 4th
that the retreat of the 5th Army was proceeding
satisfactorily, and of his fixed intention to make
the plan of battle dependent upon the co-operation
of the 5th Army. On the other hand, it followed
Galliéni's message which, as I have already said,
contemplated nothing more than a combined
attack by the 6th and British Armies. Even if we
give Galliéni the benefit of the doubt it would
seem a little extravagant to describe him in Mr.
Churchill's words as 'acting with all the sureness
and spontaneity of military genius.'[1]

Galliéni during the critical days of the Marne
nourished Maunoury's battle with all possible
energy and skill, and from the first moment when
he got news of von Kluck's flank march past Paris
he contemplated and began to prepare for a flank
attack on that general. There his credit begins and
ends. The general conception of the battle as it
was fought was from the first Joffre's and his, of
course, was the responsibility for putting that conception into execution. The final details of the
battle were proposed by d'Espérey and Wilson on

[1] Churchill, Part I, p. 26.

POSITIONS, EVENING, SEPTEMBER 5

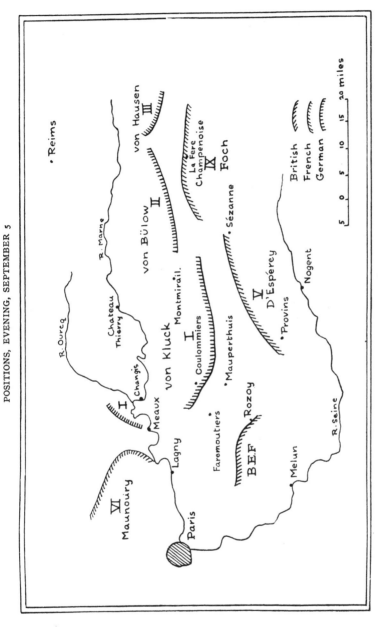

receipt of Joffre's message that the time for attack was at hand. The names of these two men have not, as far as I am aware, been even mentioned in this country in connection with the plan which stayed the German invasion of France. Actually they were representative of those elements of the Allied forces which brought about the German retreat from the Marne. For it was d'Espérey's victory over von Bülow's left at Montmirail on September 8 and the advance of the British Army to the Marne on September 9 which decided von Bülow, in consultation with Lieut.-Col. Hensch of von Moltke's staff, to order the retreat and caused Hensch to go off to von Kluck and drag that general reluctantly after von Bülow. It was the 5th Army, upon the co-operation of which in the battle Joffre had from the first insisted, which proved to be a decisive factor in the event. It was d'Espérey, not Galliéni, who fixed the date for the battle of the Marne, for it was he and he alone who could say when his army would be ready to do what Joffre required.

There remained a final step to complete the plan. So far the proposals for British action had come from staff officers, not from the British Commander-in-Chief. Therefore on September 5 Joffre went to Melun to see Sir John French and to appeal to him to throw in his army with all possible energy. This Sir John at once agreed to do, and the plan was complete.

Looking back now upon those critical days from August 25 to September 9 with all the evidence before us, it seems to me as clear as noonday that there was throughout one clear mind, with a firm and definite purpose, with broad vision, and a high courage controlling events. There are few more marked contrasts in history than that between the sickly von Moltke in his distant headquarters at Luxemburg, losing all power to control and co-ordinate the movements of his armies, and the energetic Joffre, now here, now there, on the long front, teaching the doubtful battle where to wage, ruthlessly sweeping away those, including close personal friends, whom he held not capable of dealing with a great crisis, and refusing all temptation to be drawn piecemeal into battle until he could strike ' *toutes forces réunies*.' Joffre's is indeed as fine an example of generalship in adversity as the history of war discloses, and because I believe it to be worthy of careful study I have endeavoured to rescue it from the obscurity into which it is in danger of being thrust by Mr. Churchill's brilliant pen.

After the battle was won and the great German invasion was forced back men everywhere began eagerly to speculate upon the causes of the ' miracle of the Marne.' First we were told that Foch on the evening of September 9 had broken the German centre and had hurled the Prussian Guard into the marshes of St. Gond. We know that Foch's stout-hearted defence of the French centre, and de Castelnau's equally gallant defence of Nancy, helped to make Joffre's manœuvre possible, but we know also that the German retreat had begun many hours before Foch's counter-stroke was launched. Then we were told the story, which

Mr. Churchill has repeated, that Galliéni had devised the plan of the Marne and forced his unwilling Commander-in-Chief to comply with his plan. To-day we know the facts, as I have narrated them, from the official documents.

One word in conclusion. I have referred to the attacks upon Joffre. Many of them must have been bitter to him, and none bitterer than those contained in Galliéni's memoir. Now Joffre had only to publish the messages which passed between himself and Franchet d'Espérey on September 4 to blow the Galliéni legend sky high. He did not do so because he would not say a word to injure the reputation while he was alive, or to dull the record after he was dead, of the man who had been his loved and respected chief in Madagascar. Joffre has, therefore, not only proved himself to have been a brave and skilful commander in the field but to have the mind of a great gentleman.

CHAPTER V

MR. CHURCHILL AND JUTLAND

By ADMIRAL SIR R. BACON, K.C.B., Etc.

The World Crisis, Vol. III., Part 1

Note.—All Italics are those of the writer, and do not appear in the original text from which quotations have been taken.

NOW that several thousand persons have read the latest volume of *The World Crisis*, by Mr. Winston Churchill, it is well to review, for the benefit of those who are innocent of sea affairs, that portion which deals with the Battle of Jutland.

The three volumes of *The World Crisis* are full of interest and afford much food for thought. Questions of international policy, military strategy and tactics, naval strategy and even naval tactics (I say 'even' since that subject is full of pitfalls which are apt to bog the amateur), all these are dealt with and have judgments passed on them, not only in picturesque and vivid prose, but with an assumption of knowledge and infallibility which I shall show, in a large number of instances, to be quite unwarranted.

That prodigies may exist is possible; but, humanly speaking, it is improbable that any one person should possess sufficient detailed knowledge to enable him to pass final judgments on all the intricate problems that arose during the Great War.

The fundamental virtue in a judge is the absence of bias. It is in no way derogatory to Mr. Churchill to point out, that, the vivid and energetic temperament that has distinguished his work in all the great offices of Government that he has filled, is of itself alien to calm and judicial criticism. We must further take into account that, for the major part of the war, he had taken an active part in the happenings of great events, both on the stage and behind the scenes. He had during that time expressed strong views and advocated policies, some of which were adopted while others were discarded. He had proposed operations dear to his impulsive temperament, which had been turned down by more cautious thinkers ; and lastly he had, before the war, been responsible for the appointment of some of the officers who held high command. We need not then be surprised if we find that the judgments he has so liberally meted out are tinged, and sometimes even dyed, by the dictates of an adventurous nature ; nor need we marvel that he should hold exalted views of the professional qualifications of those whom he had placed in command, and depreciate the technical abilities of those who had thwarted his most cherished schemes. He has, in short, shown himself to be, not the unbiassed judge, but rather counsel both in defence and prosecution.

Had Mr. Churchill been a man of obscure position and of less celebrity the need for refutation would not have been so great. But his world-wide reputation, and his high place among the statesmen of Europe, as well as the prestige attaching to his name, undoubtedly may cause many who read his book to accept his statements regarding the Battle of Jutland without demur, and to place credence in his ' facts.' Whether they did so or not would matter little, were it not for the fact that the reputations of officers who held high command have been assailed on assumptions that are untrue and deductions that are unwarranted. But unfortunately this, even, is not all. In his description and discussion of the Battle of Jutland the majority of his data is entirely incorrect. Indeed his account of that battle might well, without exaggeration, be described as a tissue of factual inexactitudes.

This review is not directly concerned with the doings, failures, or successes of individuals except in so far as Mr. Churchill's criticisms affect their reputations. The question as to whether this or that person was at fault, or excelled, is solely taken into review to confirm, or correct, Mr. Churchill's verdict. Nothing that has not already been published, either by the Admiralty or by critics, is taken into account ; but Mr. Churchill's omission to give due weight to these matters has often to be called into question.

Let us turn to the chapter entitled ' Jutland. The Preliminaries.'

The official records establish the following sequence of events heralding the early stages of the battle cruiser action which took place a few hours prior to the main battle :

At 2.20 p.m. Admiral Beatty was informed by the *Galatea* that enemy vessels had been sighted.
2.25. He signalled to his destroyers to take up positions for forming a screen.

2.32. He altered course, signalling the Fleet to do likewise.

2.40. The 5th Battle Squadron altered course.

From 2.32 until 3.20. Admiral Beatty steamed with the 5th Battle Squadron between ten and eight miles astern of him, without slowing down to allow them to close up.

It was not until 3.20, three-quarters of an hour after altering course, that the enemy's battle cruisers were first sighted by him.

It would naturally be expected that Mr. Churchill would take into account the major criticisms which have already been passed on the conduct of this and other phases of the battle. This he only does in some instances, in others he ignores them.

Now it had been pointed out more than a year before Mr. Churchill's book was published, that :

1. Between 2.20 and 2.32. Admiral Beatty had ample time to close up his Fleet, and still to be nearer to the enemy than he actually was at 2.32; also, that these twelve minutes should have been employed in closing up the units of his fleet. Instead of so doing these twelve minutes were wasted.

2. It was the duty of an Admiral to bring the fighting units of his fleet into action in close support of each other. This he did not do. He fell into the trap which Admiral Hipper had prepared for him, and lost thereby two cruisers and the opportunity of delivering a crushing blow to the German battle cruisers.

How does Mr. Churchill answer these two points?

1. On page 125 he states, quite loosely, that:

> six minutes steaming away from the enemy (*to close up the fleet*) might mean the loss of six thousand yards in pursuit.'

Quite so! But why should he ignore the six minutes steaming back again which would have made up the twelve minutes that were wasted?

This matter can be simply explained. If, when the signal that the enemy had been sighted was received (see diagram 1), the *Lion* had turned, say at 2.23, towards the *Barham* (the flagship of Admiral Evan Thomas) and steamed for five minutes to 2.28 and then back again for the same time, she would, allowing two minutes for the turn, have been back again in the twelve minutes to the position 2.32, or approximately to the place from which she had started. If, as she turned towards the *Barham*, she had signalled with the searchlight to that ship to close, then, if we allow three minutes for the *Barham* to have taken-in the signal and to have turned, that ship would have had nine minutes in which to close the *Lion*. This was a sufficient time to bring her into her proper station behind the sixth battle cruiser at 2.32. The main object of the turn *towards* would have been to allow all the ships to work up to full speed while the 5th Battle Squadron was closing up.

This swing 'towards and away,' *so as to work up full speed while awaiting a concentration*, is a commonplace to a tactical mind. Mr. Churchill, by dismissing this manœuvre in the curt way that he has done, leads us to doubt whether he is in any way familiar with the niceties of naval tactics.

The diagrams 1, 2, 3, 4 (facing page 126) show the matter clearly:

No. 1 shows a ' swing ' towards which has just been described. The net result would have been the fleet closed up and steaming 23 knots at 2.40.

No. 2 shows what would have happened if *Barham* had been told to close at 2.20. Net result, the fleet closed up and steaming 20 knots at 2.40.

No. 3 shows what actually happened through nothing being done for twelve minutes and then the searchlight not being used to make the turning signal. Net result, *Barham* left ten miles behind.

No. 4 shows the gain in the chase by employing No. 1 method over No. 2 method, that is by turning ' towards and away '. Net result, a gain of one and a half miles.

In the above, five minutes has been allowed for *Lion* to signal, for *Barham* to take in the signal, and then to turn. This is a reasonable allowance.

Now as regards par. 2. The reason adduced by Mr. Churchill for Admiral Beatty not closing up his fleet, although he had a whole hour in which to do it, is that which might be put forward as an excuse by a youngster in charge, for the first time, of a torpedo flotilla ; or a raw subaltern temporarily in command of a company.

Let us quote Mr. Churchill, page 125 :

> ' The doctrine that after *sufficient* force has been concentrated an admiral should delay and, at the risk of losing the whole opportunity, gather a still larger force, was one which could only be doubtfully applied even to the Battle Fleet.'

This is an excellent piece of special pleading ; the fallacy of its application is shown by the fact that the force with which Admiral Beatty rushed to meet the enemy proved to be *insufficient*.

It is not by trusting to luck, but by doing the correct thing, that unforeseen eventualities are forestalled. The history of the past, experience in the past, and the study of tactics all teach the primary necessity of closing up a fighting force before commencing an action. This was not done, and Mr. Churchill seeks further to excuse it in the following sentence on page 125 :

> ' All that impulse, all that ardour give, was no doubt present in the Admiral's mind ; but these were joined by all that the coldest science of war and the longest view of naval history proclaimed.'

This is Mr. Churchill's considered opinion in spite of Admiral Beatty being led into a trap by the utter disregard of the elementary axioms of tactics, and by the waste of twelve minutes.

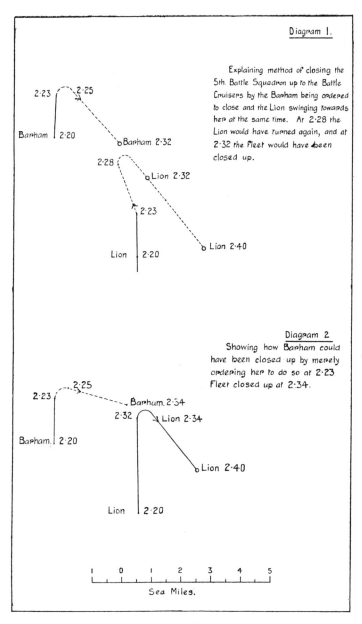

Diagram 1.

Explaining method of closing the 5th. Battle Squadron up to the Battle Cruisers by the Barham being ordered to close and the Lion swinging towards her at the same time. At 2·28 the Lion would have turned again, and at 2·32 the Fleet would have been closed up.

2·23   2·25

Barham   2·20

○Barham 2·32

2·28

○Lion 2·32

2·23

Lion   2·20

○Lion 2·40

Diagram 2
Showing how Barham could have been closed up by merely ordering her to do so at 2·23 Fleet closed up at 2·34.

2·25
2·23

Barham.   2·20

Barham. 2·54

2·32

Lion 2·34

Lion 2·40

Lion   2·20

| 0 | 2   3   4   5
Sea Miles.

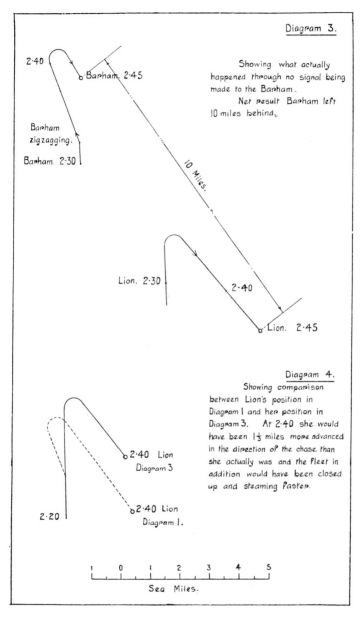

Diagram 3.

2·40

Barham. 2·45

Showing what actually
happened through no signal being
made to the Barham.
    Net result Barham left
10 miles behind.

Barham
zigzagging.

Barham. 2·30

10 Miles.

Lion. 2·30

2·40

Lion. 2·45

Diagram 4.
    Showing comparison
between Lion's position in
Diagram 1 and her position in
Diagram 3.   At 2·40 she would
have been 1½ miles more advanced
in the direction of the chase than
she actually was and the Fleet in
addition would have been closed
up and steaming faster.

2·40 Lion
Diagram 3

2·20

2·40 Lion
Diagram 1.

1   0   1   2   3   4   5
Sea Miles.

To face page 126

Mr. Churchill, however, later on recants, for we find a naive confession on page 129 that completely upsets his previous special pleading that Admiral Beatty had collected a sufficient force :

' The enemy whom he could not defeat with six ships to five are now five ships to four. Far away, all five German battle cruisers—grey smudges changing momentarily into rippling sheets of flame—are still intact and seemingly invulnerable.'

It surely must occur to every reader, taking these paragraphs together, that, after all, the teaching of naval experience in the old wars, which insists on the concentration by the Admiral of all the force possible in order to guard against the many unforeseen contingencies of a naval action, was the real and true ' longest view of naval history,' and that the disregard of such teaching cooled Admiral Beatty's ' cold science ' down to the not too useful temperature of absolute zero. In short, common sense is bound to admit that the ' cold science of war ' impelled the closing up of the 5th Battle Squadron immediately the enemy was sighted instead of wasting twelve minutes ; or, at all events, of doing so during the three-quarters of an hour that elapsed before the enemy's battle cruisers were sighted by him.

We will now turn to Mr. Churchill's apportionment of blame between Admiral Beatty and Admiral Evan Thomas for the delay in closing up the 5th Battle Squadron.

The *Barham*, the flagship of the 5th Battle Squadron, was unable to read the signal made at 2.32 p.m. to alter course owing to its having been made with flags instead of by searchlight; smoke and want of wind militated against a clear view of the flags. For the loss of these eight minutes, for which the signal staff of Admiral Beatty's flagship and not Admiral Evan Thomas must be held responsible, the latter is blamed by Mr. Churchill in thunderous periods, while Admiral Beatty, for the loss of the twelve minutes between 2.20 and 2.32 for no reason at all, receives unstinted adulation.

Let us look closely into Mr. Churchill's statements.

Admiral Evan Thomas was stationed five miles from Admiral Beatty's flagship. The reason for this appears to be that Admiral Beatty was expecting shortly to sight our Battle Fleet. The 5th Battle Squadron would, by this stationing, have been the exact distance from the battle cruisers which was laid down in the Grand Fleet Battle Orders.[1]

The formation of the Battle Cruiser Fleet was therefore what is called a ' peace cruising ' formation, that is one for convenience and not for fighting. Yet we find on page 124 that :

Admiral Evan Thomas' *general* and *dominant* orders were to keep *supporting* station five miles from the *Lion*.'

This is not a fact. There was nothing, in the signal that was made, when the 5th Battle Squadron was

[1] See diagram, p. 46 (Admiralty Narrative of Jutland).

stationed, which gave either *general* or *dominant* orders to its Admiral to keep *supporting* station. No one conversant with naval tactics, or with North Sea conditions during the war, would imagine that a squadron, stationed five miles on the English-shore side of a faster squadron, had *dominant orders* to support that squadron when it was ordered there merely by an ordinary everyday disposing signal. That they did afford a minor support to the battle cruisers is true, but only in the same sense that the main Battle Fleet, although out of sight, was supporting the battle cruisers ; or, that any two squadrons, in proximity, *de facto* give some form of support to one another.

No ! Admiral Evan Thomas was, by the signal that was made, stationed, in all probability, for the purely utilitarian purpose of being in a convenient position for taking up his station on the Battle Fleet when it was sighted.

The next thing to note is that, having once been definitely stationed on a given bearing and at a given distance from his senior officer, Admiral Evan Thomas had no right to leave that post unless circumstances arose which prevented his senior officer communicating a new order, or unless some information came to him, suddenly and un-expectedly, which was unknown to his senior officer.

Neither of these two eventualities occurred. He knew from the signal that Admiral Beatty had made to the destroyers to form a screen on a S.S.E. course that his senior officer meditated turning his cruisers to this course ; but, as no signal came to him to ' close ' or to alter course, he remained quite in the dark as to that officer's intentions regarding the 5th Battle Squadron. He has stated his dilemma as follows:

'The only way that I could account for no signal having been received by me was that the Vice-Admiral (Admiral Beatty) was going to signal another course to the 5th Battle Squadron, possibly to get the enemy's light cruisers between us. Any way, if he wished us to turn, the search-light would have done it in a moment. *It was not until the ' Tiger ' asked ' Lion ' by wireless whether the signal to turn was to be made to the ' Barham ' that the Vice-Admiral seemed to realise the situation.*'[1]

This frank statement points to the fact that Admiral Beatty, undoubtedly obsessed with thoughts of the enemy, did not observe that the 5th Battle Squadron had not altered course until his attention was called to the matter by the *Tiger;* and then, instead of slowing up to allow that squadron to close, he rushed on and left it ten miles astern.

For three-quarters of an hour Admiral Beatty steamed with his fleet straggled out, in spite of the fact that, three minutes after turning at 2.32, Commodore Goodenough in the *Galatea* signalled:

'Have sighted large amount of smoke as though from a fleet bearing E.N.E.'

At 2.45, again:

'Smoke seems to be seven vessels besides destroyers and cruisers. They have turned north.

[1] Letter to *The Times*, February 1927.

Mr. Churchill does not mention these signals, but, on the other hand, he excuses Admiral Beatty under the plea that

' The impression that every minute counted was dominant in his mind.'

How about the twelve minutes wasted between 2.20 and 2.32 ?

It may be thought that this one episode has been treated at too great a length ; this perhaps might be so if it were not for the blame cast by Mr. Churchill on Admiral Evan Thomas for Admiral Beatty's shortcomings. That, under the conditions that obtained, Admiral Evan Thomas should be made a scapegoat is cruelly unfair, and the matter is one that called for the fullest investigation.

We will now quote Mr. Churchill's crowning effort to clear Admiral Beatty at the expense of Admiral Evan Thomas, made on page 130 :

' If only they (*the 5th Battle Squadron*) had been 5000 yards closer the defeat, if not the destruction of Hipper's squadron was inevitable. That they were not 5000 yards closer was *due entirely* to their slowness in grasping the situation when *the first contact* was made with the enemy.'

A statement more at variance with the official showings could hardly have been made, especially when we remember that *the first contact* with the enemy was made at 2.20 and that Admiral Beatty did nothing until 2.32 p.m.

Mr. Churchill's naive confession, made in a

previous volume of *The World Crisis,* flashes
vividly back to the mind ; and we recognise in his
laboured defence of Admiral Beatty, and his
criticisms of another officer, the same blindness to
naval requirements and exigencies that led him to
appoint that admiral to the command of the Battle
Cruiser Squadron ' over the heads of all against
the advice of his technical advisers.'[1]

We will close this episode with examples of some
of the literary ' red herrings ' employed by Mr.
Churchill. Turn to page 122 :

' The *Galatea's* message at 2.20 *and the sound
of her guns at 2.28* were sufficient for Admiral
Beatty. German warships were at sea. At 2.32
the *Lion,* having warned her consorts of her intention, turned about again.'

Let us note, first of all, that the news at 2.20
should have been sufficient, without the guns at
2.28, for Admiral Beatty to turn ; there was no
reason to wait to hear guns before turning ; but
the insertion of this gratuitous piece of information
about the guns reduces, to the casual reader, the
apparent time of Admiral Beatty's inaction from
twelve minutes to four minutes !

Again on page 125 we find that :

' But the facts, when at 2.32 Beatty *decided
that the enemy was present in sufficient strength* to
justify turning his heavy ships about made it his
clear duty to steam at once and at the utmost
speed in their direction.'

It is here inferred that something had happened at,

[1] *World Crisis,* Vol. II, p. 87.

or immediately before, 2.32 which put Admiral Beatty in a different position from the one he was in at 2.20, and which determined him to take action. What was this 'something'? It could not have been the *Galatea's* guns, for those told him no more than he already knew about the enemy's strength. But nothing else occurred to make any difference between the facts concerning the enemy which were known at 2.20 and those known at 2.32. So that if it was Admiral Beatty's 'plain duty to steam at once and at the utmost speed' in the enemy's direction at 2.32, it was equally his plain duty to do so twelve minutes earlier. This paragraph is a good example of the literary 'red herring.'

Surely Mr. Churchill would have been on safer ground if he had been content to argue that Admiral Beatty was a fine impulsive fighter; that in the preliminary action he was obsessed with a desire to come to grips with the enemy which had escaped him in the Dogger Bank action; that he was confident that his battle cruisers could deal with the German battle cruisers without the assistance of the 5th Battle Squadron, and that for that reason he did not wait to close them up. Unfortunately his conviction as regards the result of an action between the two battle cruiser divisions was upset; and soon after the action had commenced he had sore need of the assistance of the ships of the 5th Battle Squadron, which was not forthcoming owing to his precipitate rush into battle.

If such a frank statement of the case had been made there would have been little to criticise, for the nation loves a bold leader, and welcomes a

Rupert in battle, although such a leader may, in the end, prove to be somewhat expensive. But by trying to prove that Admiral Beatty was a cautious as well as a gallant fighter, by passing blame on to the shoulders of a junior is distinctly unfair. Lord Beatty's shoulders are strong enough to stand the racket of his own actions. Why should Mr. Churchill attempt to implicate another officer ?

Mr. Churchill's description of the crisis of the battle cruiser action is vivid, but loses much of its historical value when cold common sense is applied to its fascinating and sonorous periods.

Take the following excerpt, page 129 :
' But the movements of these blind inanimate castles of steel were governed at the moment by the spirit of a single man. Had he faltered, had he taken less than a conqueror's view of the British fighting chances, all these great engines of sea power and war power would have wobbled off in meaningless disarray.'

This, let us remember, is applied to the period of the action in which four British battle cruisers and four superb British battleships were pitted against only five German battle cruisers !

What would the Country, the Navy, the World, and even Mr. Churchill himself have said if the Admiral in command of such an overwhelming force had faltered and allowed his ships to ' wobble off ' in the middle of the action ?

This paragraph is a direct insult to the spirit of the British Navy.

We will now move on to the time when the

German High Seas Fleet was sighted by the scouts of the Battle Cruiser Fleet. Admiral Scheer's trap was at once disclosed and it became forthwith necessary for the Battle Cruiser Fleet to retreat to the northward and join the Battle Fleet.

As soon as Admiral Beatty received the news from the *Galatea,* and had himself made out the approaching vessels, he signalled to his fleet to alter course to the northward. There are two things to be noted about the manner in which the turn was ordered and how it was actually carried out.

1. The signal that was made was not the one best adapted to turn all the ships away from the danger that was threatening, and which was, every minute, growing greater.
2. The 5th Battle Squadron was still steaming to the southward towards the enemy after the *Lion* had turned to the northward. The order for the Battle Squadron to turn was not given until it had passed the *Lion* steering towards the enemy on the opposite course.

The hoisting of a signal warns all ships of the Admiral's *intention.* It is improper to carry out the order conveyed until the signal is *hauled down.* ' Hauling down ' is the executive order from the Admiral to execute the signal. A signal is hoisted by the Admiral *before the moment for its execution* is due in order to convey a warning of his intention, and he hauls it down only when, in his opinion, the moment has arrived for its execution.

The signal for the 5th Battle Squadron to turn

could therefore not be obeyed until the turning signal was hauled down on board the *Lion*. It would have been highly improper for Admiral Evan Thomas to have complied with the order before the signal had been hauled down, especially as he was steaming towards the enemy.

It has been necessary to clear up this point before examining the remarks made by Mr. Churchill on page 133. The statement to be found there is here divided into paragraphs for convenience; in the book they run concurrently.

1. ' On sighting the main German Fleet Beatty had *turned about so swiftly* that his ships soon passed the 5th Battle Squadron coming up at full speed and still on their southerly course.'
2. ' As the two squadrons *ran past each other* on opposite courses the *Lion* signalled to the *Barham* (Admiral Evan Thomas' flagship) to *turn about in succession.*'
3. ' The *Lion's signal of recall* was flown at 4.48. She passed the *Barham* two miles away *with the signal still flying at* 4.53, and Rear-Admiral Evan Thomas responded to the signal *three or four minutes later.*'
4. ' Perhaps the Rear-Admiral having been slow in coming into action was inclined to be slow in coming out.'
5. ' Brief as was the interval it was sufficient at the speed at which all the ships were moving to expose the 5th Battle Squadron to action with the van of the German Fleet.'
6. ' The van was formed by the German third

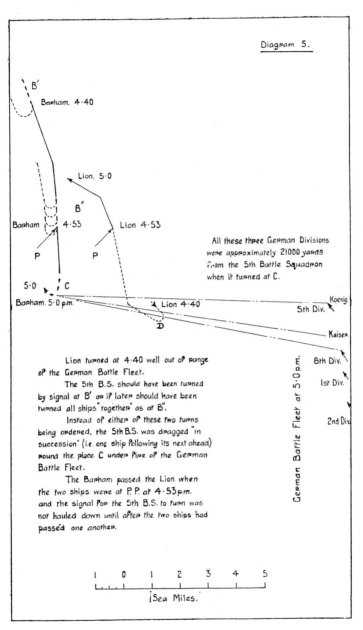

Diagram 5.

B'

Barham. 4·40

Lion. 5·0

B"

Barham 4·53   Lion 4·53

P   P

All these three German Divisions
were approximately 21000 yards
from the 5th Battle Squadron
when it turned at C.

5·0   C

Barham. 5·0 p.m.   Lion 4·40   Koenig
                                                            5th Div.

D   Kaiser

Lion turned at 4·40 well out of range
of the German Battle Fleet.
    The 5th B.S. should have been turned
by signal at B' or if later should have been
turned all ships "together" as at B".
    Instead of either of these two turns
being ordered, the 5th B.S. was dragged "in
succession" (i.e. one ship following its next ahead)
round the place C under fire of the German
Battle Fleet.
    The Barham passed the Lion when
the two ships were at P.P. at 4·53 p.m.
and the signal for the 5th B.S. to turn was
not hauled down until after the two ships had
passed one another.

6th Div.

1st Div.

2nd Div.

German Battle Fleet at 5·0 p.m.

1   0   1   2   3   4   5

Sea Miles.

To face page 136

squadron comprising the *Königs* and the *Kaisers*, the strongest and the newest vessels in the German Navy. The four *Queen Elizabeths* were now subjected to a tremendous fire concentrated on the point where each turned in succession.'

If the English language means anything, the impression intended to be conveyed by paragraphs 3 and 4 is that the damage done to the 5th Battle Squadron was owing to Admiral Evan Thomas' delay before obeying Admiral Beatty's signal.

Now for the facts which probably are not apparent to the general reader. To begin with, Admiral Beatty made the wrong signal. He should have turned all the ships of the 5th Battle Squadron *together*, either at B″ or B″, diagram 5, in the same way that Admiral Scheer turned his fleet later on to escape from our Battle Fleet.

Instead of turning all his ships *together*, the manœuvre that later on is belauded by Mr. Churchill when adopted by Admiral Scheer, Admiral Beatty first turned his cruisers ' in succession ' round a pivot (position D)[1], and then by the signal he made caused the 5th Battle Squadron similarly to turn round a point, C, on which the fire of the German van was concentrated.

Moreover, Mr. Churchill states that the signal to the *Barham* was *kept flying* until after she had passed Admiral Beatty's cruisers ; but he does not mention at what time the signal was *hauled down*,

[1] As there was plenty of time in hand there was no reason that the Battle Cruisers should not have been turned *in succession*. The fact that this was done is merely here recorded.

or that Admiral Evan Thomas obeyed the signal as soon as it was hauled down. In paragraph 3 of his statement above he remarks that :

'She passed the *Barham* with the signal still flying at 4.53, and Rear-Admiral Evan Thomas responded to the signal three or four minutes later.

What he fails, however, to state is that this delay was due to the signal not being hauled down on board the *Lion*.

The average civilian would probably not appreciate that a signal is not obeyed until it is hauled down, he would therefore naturally read Mr. Churchill's incomplete statement as meaning that Admiral Evan Thomas did not immediately obey the signal but wasted three or four minutes.

As a matter of history, when the draft of the Official Narrative, which had been compiled by the Naval Staff when Lord Beatty was Chief of the Staff, was sent to Admiral Evan Thomas for his remarks, he pointed out the above facts about the signal to turn. It was because the Admiralty refused to make the necessary corrections in the Narrative that Admiral Jellicoe made a strong protest that was merely inserted as a footnote to that publication.

Note also, how by carelessly calling the signal 'the signal to turn' in one case, and the 'signal of recall' immediately afterwards, the fact that 'the signal to turn' was left flying until after the *Barham* had passed the *Lion* is liable to be overlooked by the casual reader. Moreover, as the 'general recall' is acted on and obeyed as soon as it is *seen*, and the signal 'to turn' is not complied with until after it has been hauled down, the professional reader even, unless on his guard, might be betrayed into the belief that Admiral Evan Thomas did not obey the signal as promptly as he should have done.

The remark in paragraph 4 is uncalled for and undeserved.

From this sifting of Mr. Churchill's 'facts' it has become clear that the blame for any damage done to the 5th Battle Squadron must be placed entirely on Admiral Beatty's shoulders. Mr. Churchill's attempt to fix it on to the shoulders of Admiral Evan Thomas merely shows his want of insight into naval tactics, and reflects on his judgment. Well might Admiral Evan Thomas apostrophise Mr. Churchill, in his dual capacity of Chancellor of the Exchequer and critic, in the words of Iago :

Who steals my purse steals trash; 'tis something, nothing;
'Twas mine, 'tis his, and has been slave to thousands;
But he, that filches from me my good name,
Robs me of that, which not enriches him,
And makes me poor indeed.

We confess to feeling considerable regret that Mr. Churchill did not treat, in vivid prose, the dramatic change in rôle that came over the Battle Cruiser Fleet the instant that the German High Seas Fleet was sighted at 4.33 p.m. In the flash of a second the duties and functions of the Battle Cruiser Fleet underwent a complete change. One second before that momentous event they were a fleet fighting the enemy to the death, with no other preoccupation than, at all hazards, to sink and destroy. One second after the news that the German High Seas Fleet had been sighted was flashed to the Admiral, they became merely the scouting force of the Battle Fleet, and their one object became to give the Commander-in-Chief all the information possible to ensure his meeting the enemy under the most favourable conditions. Admiral Beatty was no longer a Commander-in-Chief, he became the Admiral of the scouting squadron, to whom fighting was but a subsidiary function to be indulged in merely to prevent the enemy's cruisers sighting our Fleet, or so long as it did not interfere with the primary duty of scouting. Of this sudden transformation nothing, unfortunately, is said. We are told, however, that :

> ' Beatty tried to lead Hipper and the German Fleet up to Jellicoe.'

Let us examine this assertion in the light of facts. What actually did Admiral Beatty do ? He ran back to the Battle Fleet out of sight of the German High Seas Fleet, carrying on a desultory game of long bowls with the German battle cruisers. If his first object had been, as Mr. Churchill states, to lead the German High Seas Fleet up to Jellicoe he would surely, at all costs, have remained in sight of them as a bait to draw them on. As it was the 5th Battle Squadron formed the bait, and this only because, at maximum speed, they could not sufficiently outpace the fast battleships of the enemy. The fact was that the German Battle

Fleet required no leading. They chased our battle cruisers with a will.

Let us now pass to the junction of the battle cruisers and the Grand Battle Fleet. It is well here to be quite clear and emphatic. Admiral Beatty after sighting the German Battle Fleet had become the Admiral commanding the main scouting force of the Grand Fleet.

It was his duty to convey exact information to his Commander-in-Chief. But this is precisely what he failed to do. When he arrived in sight of the *Iron Duke* (Admiral Jellicoe's flagship), after having lost sight of the German High Seas Fleet, Admiral Jellicoe signalled at 6.01 p.m. : ' Where is the enemy's Battle Fleet ? ' Admiral Beatty did not know. He had, so to speak, mislaid them. He could give no reply.

Although he had thirteen light cruisers under his command, he had not thrown out any of these to form connecting links for passing information by visual signals of the movements of the German Battle Fleet to the British Battle Fleet.

For a *whole quarter of an hour* Admiral Jellicoe could get no answer from Admiral Beatty except that the German battle cruisers bore S.E. As if it mattered a brass farthing to Admiral Jellicoe how the German battle *cruisers* bore ! What Admiral Jellicoe wanted to know, and what he should have been able to learn from Admiral Beatty, was where the German Battle *Fleet* was. As a matter of fact they were on a totally different bearing from that of their battle cruisers.

In this manner the valuable quarter of an hour

which should have been available to Admiral Jellicoe to swing the columns of the Battle Fleet, so as to deploy to the best advantage to meet the enemy, was lost through Admiral Beatty failing to realise the functions for which his Cruiser Fleet mainly existed.

Now how does Mr. Churchill deal with this matter?

In a most bare-faced manner he attempts to take the onus for scouting off the shoulders of the Scouting Admiral and put it on to those of the Admiral commanding the Battle Fleet!

Let us quote Mr. Churchill's views of what Admiral Jellicoe should have done. These, being lengthy, are divided into paragraphs for simplicity of treatment. On page 142 we find :

1. ' Apart from the fourteen light cruisers detached with Admiral Beatty's advanced force Jellicoe had reserved for his own special use *four* of the very latest *Caroline* class of light cruiser.

2. ' He had besides the eight armoured cruisers of the pre-Dreadnought era. At the first alarm he ordered these old vessels to increase to full speed and cover his front, but as they could not steam more than *twenty knots* and he was himself making eighteen and rising twenty they did not appreciably draw ahead of him in these important two hours.

3. ' In two hours the *Carolines* in a fan formation could easily have gained fifteen miles from the *Iron Duke* in the general direction of the enemy. The *Carolines* themselves at

this time could see at least seven miles. Then the *Commander-in-Chief, had he so wished,* could have had more than twenty miles accurate notice by visual signal of the position and line of advance of the German Fleet.'

We will take these paragraphs in sequence and show the errors in them.

1. There were five *Carolines* with Admiral Jellicoe, not four as stated.

2. The armoured cruisers could steam twenty-two and a half and twenty-three knots, not twenty as stated; they were therefore at least four and a half to two and a half knots faster than the speeds at which the Battle Fleet was steaming during the two hours. The true reason why they did not reach the position assigned to them was, not because their speed was as slow as Mr. Churchill imagines it to have been, but because after 4 p.m. the weather thickened and the ships had to close one another to keep visual touch. This meant that the wing ships had to ' close in ' on diagonal courses, and the ' advance ' of the whole screen was delayed.

3. Even if the speed of the armoured cruisers had been as low as that on which Mr. Churchill bases his argument, there still was no reason for sending the *Carolines* ahead at 3.10 instead of the armoured cruisers, for the simple fact, which he appears to have overlooked, that at that time the 3rd Battle Cruiser Squadron with two light cruisers was stationed

twenty miles ahead of the Battle Fleet, in the very position to which Mr. Churchill suggests that Admiral Jellicoe should have sent the *Carolines*. It is obvious therefore that it would have been useless from every point of view to have sent the *Carolines* ahead, especially as the only enemy reported at sea at 3.10 (the time that the armoured cruisers were sent ahead) was a German light cruiser force, with which the armoured cruisers and the two light cruisers were perfectly able to deal.

It is often difficult to follow Mr. Churchill's arguments because of the inaccuracies they contain; the above is an example, for there are no less than three in the quoted paragraphs, namely the speed of the armoured cruisers is incorrect, the number of *Carolines* under Admiral Jellicoe is misstated, the time at which the armoured cruisers were sent forward was not 'at the first alarm' but fifty minutes after the first alarm. But the really important point that emerges, is that the whole of Mr. Churchill's elaborate argument, as to what the Commander-in-Chief of the Grand Fleet should have done, is based on an inaccurate estimate of the speed of the armoured cruisers and an oversight as to the position of the 3rd Battle Cruiser Squadron at 3.10 p.m.

We must remember, further, that the Admiralty had informed Admiral Jellicoe at noon that the German High Seas Fleet was still in the Jade. If the *Carolines* had been sent ahead at 4.38, when for the first time it was known, or even suspected, that the German High Seas Fleet was at sea, they could only have arrived ten to twelve miles ahead of our Battle Fleet. The visibility for signalling purposes at that time was only five miles, so that, as a matter of fact, the westernmost *Caroline* would only have been in the position then occupied by the *Black Prince*. Moreover, as events turned out, Admiral Beatty had failed to keep in touch with the German Battle Fleet ; so, even if the *Carolines* had, by some miraculous impossibility, sighted the *Lion* they could have got no information out of her. Their queries might, however, have awakened the Admiral to a sense of his scouting responsibilities. As regards paragraph 3, no reader can fail to regret Mr. Churchill's insinuation contained in the words ' had he so wished.' Incompetence is the very least that this could imply.

To sum up : Mr. Churchill absolves the Scouting Admiral for his failure in his scouting duties and, in order to clear him, tries to throw the blame on the Commander-in-Chief of the Battle Fleet, quite failing to appreciate that even if he could show that the Commander-in-Chief could have assisted Admiral Beatty to pass him important news of the exact position of the enemy's Fleet, this did not in any way relieve the latter of his responsibilities as Admiral in command of the scouting forces of the Grand Fleet.

Further, in instructing the world as to what the Commander-in-Chief should have done, he bases his theory on incorrect data, and fails to appreciate the effect that the rapidly thickening haze had on the disposition of the outposts of the Battle Fleet.

This is a good example of the errors an amateur is liable to drop into when attempting to deal with naval tactics. We shall, however, see worse attempts later on.

Why, again, could not Mr. Churchill look on this episode in a commonsense way? He could have pointed out that Admiral Beatty allowed his fighting instincts to dull his appreciation of the scouting duties of his fleet. His attention was undoubtedly fixed on his old enemy, the German Battle Cruiser Squadron, and so the scouting suffered. Everyone would recognise that with an impulsive fighter the meticulous care of a more stable temperament is apt to be lost; it is rare to find both qualities evenly balanced. This could be well understood, but to try and persuade the people of this country that the Commander-in-Chief of the Battle Fleet was responsible for the scouting failure of his Scouting Admiral is merely to tax severely their patience, and impose a heavy strain on their credulity.

We now come to subject-matter that is positively entertaining. Mr. Churchill leaves cruiser tactics and, taking on the rôle of naval battle-tactician, lays down an alternative tactic that should have been used in the deployment of the Battle Fleet, and expresses astonishment that Admiral Jellicoe should

'never have attempted to deal with this alternative in any of his accounts and explanations of his actions.'

How naive! Did it never occur to Mr. Churchill

that it was never worthy even of the terse comment passed on it by the authors of the German Official History of the war? But I am anticipating.

The Battle Fleet is now about to deploy, and we have the option either of visiting Mr. Churchill, as he sits in an armchair in his well-lighted and commodious library, with all the many charts of Jutland showing the positions of both fleets and all their auxiliaries spread out before him, the result of the labour of many brains during several years of post-war work, where with pencil, compasses, protractor, and eraser he satisfies himself as to what Admiral Churchill would have done had he commanded the British Fleet eleven years earlier; or, of standing with Admiral Jellicoe on the bridge of the *Iron Duke*, in the mist and haze of the North Sea, with the guns of the enemy heard but difficult to locate, with the battle cruisers having steamed into sight on a bearing quite different from that which was expected, and their Admiral unable to supply him with the much-needed information of the enemy's position. All is haze and uncertainty, seconds are ticking by and no information is forthcoming as to their exact position. Deploy he must, but how? How best to meet the enemy of whose exact position he should have been, but has not been, informed?

The two positions are so different that we must in turn visit both. Let us, to begin with, take the comfortable library.

The British Battle Fleet was steaming down fast to the southward in six parallel lines like the teeth of a comb, each tooth being composed of a division of four ships. The total distance between the extreme right and left-hand tooth was five miles. In order to form line-of-battle any one of the six divisions could have been told to steam straight on, and the other divisions ordered to form astern of it, in any order that the Admiral might wish. Considerable controversy has raged round the question as to which was the best division to 'form' on. Mr. Churchill advocates a division which does not commend itself to the naval officer.

Turn to page 137, where we find the following accurate summary of the situation :

'He (*Admiral Scheer*) had no intention of fighting a battle against the whole British Fleet. He was under no illusions about the relative strength of the rival batteries. Nothing could be more clownish than to draw up his fleet on parallel courses with an opponent firing twice his weight of metal and manned by a personnel whose science, seamanship, and fortitude commanded his sincere respect. *He had not come out with any idea of fighting a pitched battle.* He had never intended to fight at a hopeless disadvantage.'

With this statement of the case every one will agree. Let us see how it bears on the advantages or disadvantages of any special form of deployment.

The main points to keep in mind are that (1) the moment Admiral Scheer sighted our Battle Fleet he would have turned and fled, unless he found himself in a position of considerable tactical advantage[1]; and (2) he would have sighted our Battle Fleet the same distance off whichever column the Grand Fleet had deployed on, since the range of visibility was the same in every class of deployment. It did not matter in the slightest if he sighted the leading battleships of our fleet right ahead or on his bow, in either case he would have turned and run straight away from them.

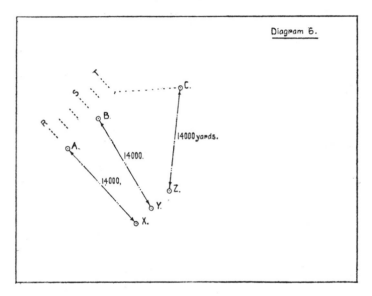

Diagram 6.

Let this be thoroughly understood as it is a point that all the many lay tacticians have missed.

Look at diagram 6. If Admiral Jellicoe had deployed on the division R the leading ship of that division would have been sighted by Admiral Scheer at A when he (Scheer) was at X.

If the deployment had been, as Mr. Churchill

---

[1] Since writing the above, an article by Admiral Scheer has appeared in the *Fortnightly* fully confirming the fact that he would have fought if he could have placed his fleet in a position of advantage, but not otherwise.

suggests, on the division S Admiral Scheer would have sighted the leading ship at B when he was at Y. The deployment actually took place on the division T, and he sighted the ships of our Battle Fleet at C when he was at Z.

The distance at which he would have sighted the ships in the first two cases would, of course, have been the same as that at which he did actually sight our fleet in the third case, namely about 14,000 yards.

He would without doubt have turned at Y and perhaps also at X for exactly the same reason that he did at Z, namely to run *straight* away from our fleet. When he turned, our fleet would have been *no nearer* to him had it deployed on R and S than when it deployed on T.

Yet on page 141 in diagram 11 Mr. Churchill states as regards the deployment on S, which is the one that he recommends :

'this deployment would have placed the British line about 4000 yards nearer the German Fleet.'

It would have done nothing of the sort. The visibility in the North Sea could not have been affected by the manœuvre, however it might have been performed.

On page 148 he is more grasping and at the same time more obscure! Here he claims for his manœuvre, which he modestly calls the 'sure, prudent, glorious, and middle course,' that

'he (Jellicoe) would have had three miles and ten minutes more to spare than if he had deployed on the wing towards the enemy.'

We confess to not grasping what ' *three miles and ten minutes more to spare* ' means. But if we understand him at all, his claim has risen from four thousand yards to three miles, which is equivalent to six thousand yards. Perhaps the ' ten minutes ' means ten minutes earlier contact with the German Fleet.

Now since not one of these three methods of deployment ensured our fleet being nearer to the enemy's fleet than either of the other two, what was the virtue of any one deployment over another ?

Let us look at diagram 7.

In the case of deployment on R there was a great danger of the German Fleet overlapping the head of our line (crossing its T) which was the one main position of disadvantage in which a fleet can be placed. If this comes to pass, the leading ship of the line that is advancing along the upright stroke of the T comes under the fire of the broadsides of all the ships steaming along the top bar of the T, while she herself is only able to reply with her right-ahead fire. She is forced to turn parallel to the cross-bar (as the *Marlborough* would have had to have done at A), and, as every succeeding ship turns, each is unmercifully strafed at the pivot between B and A, a spot of which the enemy has obtained the exact range.

The ' sure, prudent, and glorious middle course of deploying on S presented no advantage to either side as regards ' crossing the T.' See diagram 8. Both fleets could have used their broadside guns.

The deployment on the division T reversed the

advantage described in the deployment on R by giving it to the British instead of the German Fleet; we thereby crossed the enemy's T and strafed them with considerable effect. See diagram 9.

But there was yet another great advantage which was gained by deploying on the division T: this was, that when Admiral Scheer turned and ran *straight away* from our fleet when he was at Z, the *straight away* led him towards *England*, as Mr. Churchill points out on page 151. At either X or Y the course *straight away* from our fleet was the direct course for the German coast. If he had sighted our ships at X or Y he would have turned and run straight away and been no more seen, either that day or the next morning.

Admiral Jellicoe naturally dismissed Mr. Churchill's ' sure, prudent, glorious, and middle course since, while offering no advantage, it would have merely ' bunched ' the fleet badly in case of torpedo attack. He therefore deployed on the division T with the result that he drove the German Fleet away from their own shores.[1] He brought his fleet just as *near* to the German Fleet as he could have done by any other method, and by not deploying on the R division he saved the leading ships of the *Marlborough* (R) division from a severe and unnecessary handling by the *König* and *Kaiser* Dreadnoughts.

It is very easy for any one dealing for the first time with problems of naval tactics to drop into

---

[1] The *Invincible*, ahead of our Battle Fleet, was believed by Admiral Scheer to be leading our line of battleships, which again headed him away from his own ports.

Diagram 7.

Deploying on Marlborough Division. (R in Diagram 6.)

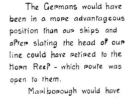

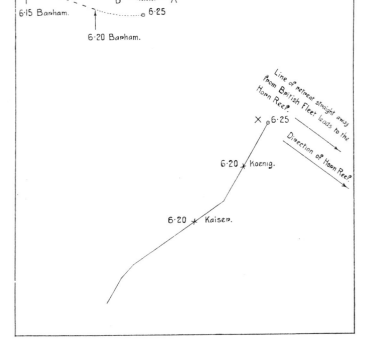

The Germans would have been in a more advantageous position than our ships and after slating the head of our line could have retired to the Horn Reef - which route was open to them.

Marlborough would have been forced to turn from B to A. All the ships following her would have come under fire during the turn.

To face page 152

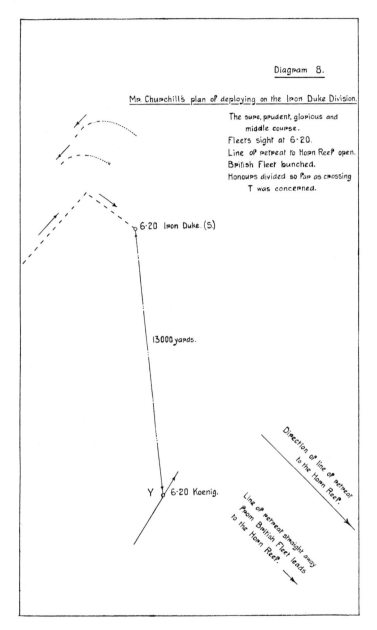

Diagram 8.

Mr. Churchill's plan of deploying on the Iron Duke Division.

The sure, prudent, glorious and
middle course.
Fleets sight at 6·20.
Line of retreat to Horn Reef open.
British Fleet bunched.
Honours divided so far as crossing
T was concerned.

6·20 Iron Duke. (5.)

13000 yards.

Y 6·20 Koenig.

Direction of line of retreat
to the Horn Reef.

Line of retreat straight away
from British Fleet leads
to the Horn Reef.

To face page 152

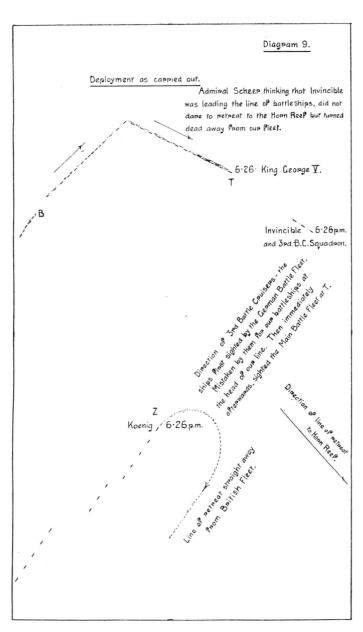

Diagram 9.

Deployment as carried out.

Admiral Scheer thinking that Invincible was leading the line of battleships, did not dare to retreat to the Horn Reef but turned dead away from our Fleet.

6·26 King George V.
T

B

Invincible ✕ 6·26 p.m.
and 3rd B.C. Squadron.

Direction of 3rd Battle Cruisers - the ships first sighted by the German Battle Fleet. Mistaken by them for our battleships at the head of our line. Then immediately afterwards, sighted the Main Battle Fleet at T.

Direction of line of retreat to Horn Reef.

Z
Koenig ✕ 6·26 p.m.

Line of retreat straight away from British Fleet.

To face page 152

mistakes like the above over which Mr. Churchill has come to grief.

But the inaccuracies on this matter of deployment that we find in this volume do not stop here. On page 147 we find :

> Our present knowledge leads to the conclusion that he (Jellicoe) could have deployed on the starboard wing without misadventure.'

Our present knowledge shows that such a deployment would have caused considerable risk to the *Marlborough* division, as the Germans were virtually across the *Marlborough's* T. See diagram 7.

He then continues :

> ' The 5th Battle Squadron, with its unequalled guns, armour, and speed, was in fact *about* to take the van ahead of the *Marlborough.'*

About to take is a very different thing from *having taken*. It would have had to steam under fire for at least ten minutes before it could have arrived into station ahead of the *Marlborough,* and during the whole of that time its ships would have masked the fire of the guns of the *Marlborough* division and been subjected to a heavy concentration of fire from practically the whole of the *König* and *Kaiser* divisions of seven ships.

In conclusion, surely a telling argument against the deployment on the starboard or R division, so dear to the amateur tactician, is the verdict of the German Naval Staff in their Official History of the war. These officers had no axes to grind, and their considered opinion, which is free from all bias, is as follows :

'One must agree with the British leader (Jellicoe) that had he acted in this way (i.e. deploying on the starboard wing division) he would in fact have led his ships into a position which would have been only too welcome to the German Fleet.'

As regards Mr. Churchill's 'sure, prudent, and glorious middle course' the same high authority sweeps this aside for a reason which I prefer not to advance, namely that it was too complicated a manœuvre to have been undertaken in the presence of an enemy. Perhaps Mr. Churchill might feel inclined, in turn, to sweep aside this verdict and, with a pardonable prejudice for all things British, say, 'Oh yes, but the German officers were not so highly trained as ours and might therefore naturally shirk a manœuvre which was well within the capacity of our fleet.' In case this might be his reply we would point out that on page 136, where he glorifies the training of the German High Seas Fleet at the expense of the Grand Fleet under Admiral Jellicoe, he remarks:

'The Germans, following the Army system of command, had foreseen before the war that the intelligent co-operation of subordinates, who know thoroughly the views and spirit of their Chief, must be substituted in a fleet action for a rigid and centralised control.'

The manœuvre recommended by Mr. Churchill was essentially one in which *the intelligent co-operation of subordinates was substituted for a rigid and centralised control,* since each Divisional Commander would have taken charge of, and manœu-vred, his division by signal. The German naval authorities therefore, according to his own show-ing, should have been thoroughly good judges of the manœuvre, yet their verdict is unhesitatingly adverse to it.

Our naval officers do not condemn it on the same grounds to the same extent, but there is no doubt that it is a manœuvre that any Admiral would hesitate to carry out in close proximity to an enemy, unless it held out, at the moment, far greater advantages than on this occasion were likely to accrue.

A glance at Mr. Churchill's diagram in the *World Crisis* will show that the ships of the fleet would have been ' bunched ' up, and very vulner-able to torpedo attack had one been launched against them during twelve of the eighteen minutes or so that it would have taken to carry out the deployment on the column that he has advocated.

Mr. Churchill now proceeds to tell us what the Commander-in-Chief should alternatively have ordered the 5th Battle Squadron to do while the fleet was deploying. Here he gets completely out of his depth. On page 149 we find :

' His (Jellicoe's) cautious deployment on the outer wing made it more imperative to make sure of the enemy being brought to action. To do this he had *only* to tell the four *Queen Eliza-beths* of the 5th Battle Squadron . . . to attack separately on the *disengaged side* of the enemy. . . . They were eight or nine knots faster than Scheer's fleet as *long as it remained united.'*

First of all let us note there were only three of the 5th Battle Squadron left at 6.20. *Warspite* was out of action.

If Mr. Churchill had used his compasses he would have discovered that Admiral Jellicoe was more than three thousand yards out of sight of the German Fleet when he made the signal to deploy. He was hardly, therefore, in a position to order one of his divisions to attack an enemy whom he could not see, and of whose exact position he was in doubt. Moreover, as the ships of the 5th Battle Squadron were at that time on the *engaged* side of the enemy, it would have been impossible for them to get through the German Fleet to its disengaged side. If they had attempted to go round it they would have had to steam some forty miles, and had they ever arrived at so impossible a position as the one Mr. Churchill suggests they would have had the broadsides of the whole of the German Dreadnought fleet to contend with!

So we find that Mr. Churchill in reality suggests that Admiral Jellicoe should have ordered one of his divisions, whose strength is wrongly stated, to attack the disengaged side of an enemy whom he could not see, and whose position he did not know, and whose disengaged side it was impossible to get at.

But with Mr. Churchill unjustifiable assumption follows fast on the heels of impossible suggestion. For further on he assigns still further duties to the 5th Battle Squadron. We read :

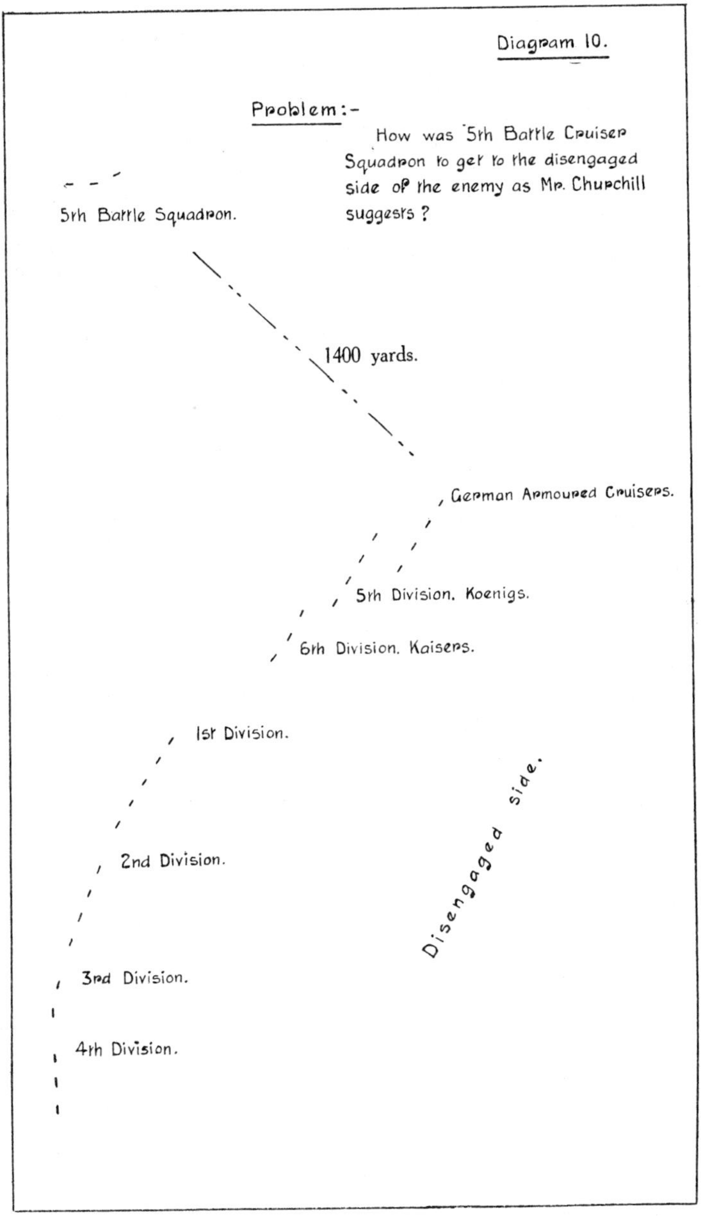

Diagram 10.

Problem :-

How was 5th Battle Cruiser
Squadron to get to the disengaged
side of the enemy as Mr. Churchill
suggests ?

5th Battle Squadron.

1400 yards.

German Armoured Cruisers.

5th Division. Koenigs.

6th Division. Kaisers.

1st Division.

2nd Division.

Disengaged side.

3rd Division.

4th Division.

To face page 156

' They (the 5th Battle Squadron) could at any moment if too hard pressed break off the action. Thus assured, what could be easier than for them to swoop round on the old *Deutschland* Squadron and cripple or destroy two or three of these ships in a few minutes ? '

Thus Mr. Churchill wrote from his arm-chair in the clear atmosphere of his library, with the post-war charts spread on the table. It never seems to have struck him, seeing as he did the whole of the German dispositions laid out before him, that neither Admiral Jellicoe nor Admiral Evan Thomas nor anyone else in the Grand Fleet had any knowledge where exactly the *Deutschlands* were. None of the enemy battleships except the leading division of German Dreadnoughts could be seen by Admiral Evan Thomas, still less by Admiral Jellicoe, who at that moment could see none of the enemy's ships, nor had any but these few ships been seen by anyone in the Battle Fleet.

What sort of a naval idiot would Admiral Evan Thomas have been thought, and Admiral Jellicoe been accused of being, if, without knowing where the *Deutschlands* were, either of them had ordered a wild goose chase on the part of the 5th Battle Squadron past the flank of sixteen German Dreadnoughts to attack ships which they could not see, and incidentally in so doing have separated that squadron several miles from the main fleet ?

If before criticising the actions of the Commander-in-Chief of the Grand Fleet at any particular phase of the action Mr. Churchill had first prepared a chart or, better still, enlisted the services of some competent person to do so for him, which chart excluded all of the enemy's forces except those that were visible to the Commander-in-Chief at the particular moment in question, he would have been less likely to have fallen into errors of the same class as those with which we have been dealing. He would then not have pored over a post-war chart that set forth the whole dispositions of the enemy, and based his criticisms on the assumption that the Commander-in-Chief was blessed with eyes that could penetrate more than five miles beyond normal human vision.

The next important matters to note are Mr. Churchill's arguments in favour of independent action on the part of the various units of the fleet. Let us quote him on this matter, page 136 :

> ' Neither admiration nor agreement can adhere to the system and training which he (Admiral Jellicoe) had developed in his fleet. Everything was centralised in the flagship, and all initiative, except in avoiding torpedo attack, was denied to the leaders of squadrons and divisions.'

Neither admiration nor agreement can adhere to this statement in the light of the following extracts from the Grand Fleet Battle Orders which Mr. Churchill could have consulted had he so wished. There is nothing in these extracts that can in any way be looked on as confidential.

The opening paragraph of these orders, which were in force at the Battle of Jutland, read as follows :

' The Commander-in-Chief controls the whole Battle Fleet BEFORE deployment and ON deployment except in the case of low visibility.

' He cannot be certain AFTER deployment of being able to control the movements of three Battle Squadrons when steaming fast and making much funnel smoke : with the noise and smoke of battle added, the practicability of exercising general control will be still further reduced.

' It therefore becomes necessary to decentralise command to the fullest extent possible, and the Vice-Admirals commanding squadrons have discretionary power to manœuvre their squadrons independently while conforming generally to the movements of the Commander-in-Chief and complying with his known intentions. As the Commander-in-Chief is in the centre he will ordinarily control the movements of the 4th Battle Squadron should separate action by that squadron become necessary, but as the fleet is manœuvred by divisions in the fifth organisation after deployment the Vice-Admiral 4th Battle Squadron will control the movements of his division, conforming generally to the movements of the division led by the Commander-in-Chief, unless any contrary directions are given. Similarly the Rear-Admirals 1st and 2nd Battle Squadrons control the movements of their divisions unless they receive directions from the Commander-in-Chief or the Vice-Admirals of their squadrons.'

Although paragraph 3 states that ' the ruling

principle is that the Dreadnought fleet as a whole keeps together, attempted attacks by a division or squadron on a portion of the enemy line being avoided as being liable to lead to the isolation of the ships which attempt the movement,' this did not deny initiative in other respects as the following paragraphs show.

'There are several conditions which may call for separate action on the part of commanders of squadrons and divisions.' Among the conditions was 'a movement of one of the enemy's divisions necessitating a counter on our part, such as an attack on the rear or attempt to close for the purpose of firing torpedoes, etc.'

There were also certain instructions as to dealing with the German Battle Fleet if it divided, which mentioned that commanders of squadrons and divisions might have to act independently.

It was stated that the 3rd Battle Squadron (which, however, was detached before the battle) was to be manœuvred by the Vice-Admiral commanding independently of the Dreadnought fleet.

A final paragraph laid down that whenever junior flag officers or captains find themselves without special directions during an action, either from inability to make out or receive the Admiral's signals or from unforeseen circumstances rendering previous orders inapplicable, they are to act as their judgment shall dictate in making every effort to damage the enemy. It is difficult to see how Admiral Jellicoe could have given wider discretionary freedom to his juniors without a general action developing into a mass of small engagements swayed by the idiosyncrasies and varying temperaments of the commanders of the divisions.

How was it possible for Mr. Churchill to be so misinformed as to make a statement so palpably at variance with fact ? Mr. Churchill has indeed been badly served by his naval advisers, who should have pointed out to him these very obvious mistakes. He was kind in not mentioning their names in the preface to his volumes.[1]

But the above is by no means his only erroneous statement on the matter. We find, page 136 :

' A ceaseless stream of signals from the flagship was therefore required to regulate the movements and the distribution of the fire.'

This was not so. Between 6.15, after the signal to deploy had been made, up to 9.11, when the fleet turned to a southerly course for the night (apart from signals giving the course and speed of the flagship, which would have been necessary if the fleet had been divided into separate manœuvring squadrons), twenty-four signals only were made giving orders for the movements of the fleet. The distribution of fire was left to the Admirals commanding the divisions. Twenty-four signals in approximately three hours, or two signals every quarter of an hour, can scarcely be called a ' ceaseless stream.'[2]

Mr. Churchill continues :

' These signals prescribed the course and speed

[1] See Preface to *The World Crisis*, Vol. III.
[2] Sixteen signals were made between these hours informing the Fleet generally of the course and speed of the *Iron Duke*. But these would have been necessary however little or much the Fleet had been decentralised.

of every ship as well as every manœuvring turn.'

Anyone reading this would surely imagine that the whole of the twenty-seven battleships had a ceaseless stream of signals made to each of them prescribing their courses. Needless to say Mr. Churchill meant nothing of the sort. What he intended to convey was, that a single three-flag signal would order all the leaders of divisions to turn in a certain direction : the ships behind them would follow their leaders round. A single three-flag signal would control the whole movement.

This is what Mr. Churchill must have meant. It is a pity therefore that he, who when he likes can be so very explicit, should apparently at times be so careless as to the impression he conveys to a public mainly ignorant of naval matters.

A little later, when he wishes to convey the impression that the German system of fleet control was superior to that of the Grand Fleet, we read in support of the argument, page 136 :

' At this moment (*the approach of the two fleets before sighting each other*) the line in which they were approaching was in fact three self-contained, independently moving squadrons following one another.'

As a matter of fact this was not so. As we have already seen, during the run north after 4.33 p.m. Admiral Scheer had chased the 5th Battle Squadron; that is, he had taken his ships along at their utmost speed. This led naturally to his squadrons opening out, since each squadron was composed of ships of approximately the same speed, but each squadron varied in speed from the other two. The result was that certain gaps developed between the squadrons, but they still remained a combined fleet. Indeed Mr. Churchill himself confirms this on page 151 :

> ' He (Scheer) therefore at 6.35, with the utmost promptitude, turned his whole fleet about, every ship turning simultaneously.'

If this was not control of the fleet by one man, nothing in this world can come under that definition. Had the fleet been made up of ' independently moving squadrons ' Admiral Scheer would perforce have signalled to the leaders of the individual squadrons to turn their squadrons. Nothing of the sort was done ; he *turned his whole fleet, every ship turning simultaneously.*

There is yet another example of the vagueness of Mr. Churchill's knowledge of naval tactics. On page 137 we find a wholehearted admiration of Admiral Scheer's ' turn-about ' movement when in an awkward predicament. This, we may explain for the benefit of those who are not versed in the manœuvres of a fleet, was one of the simplest of all manœuvres, a simple ' turn together ' to a course indicated by a signal. If to-morrow batches of battleships, cruisers, or destroyers were taken haphazard and formed into separate fleets, and each one put into any reasonable ' kink or disorder,' then, if the same order was given, there is no doubt that all the vessels would come triumphantly out of the ordeal. A turn ' together ' is a commonplace in naval tactics, even if the line of ships to which it addressed has a bend or angle in it.

We must now pass to the actual contact between the two Battle Fleets at 6.25. In the opening paragraph, on page 152, where Mr. Churchill deals with this encounter, he makes an inexcusable statement. He describes the hasty retreat of Von Scheer's battleships, and adds :

> ' Jellicoe, threatened by the torpedo stream, turned away according to his long-resolved policy.'

Neither at this time, nor even approximately at this time, did Admiral Jellicoe turn away from a torpedo attack. No attack by destroyers appeared from the *Iron Duke* to be in course of preparation. On the other hand, two turns were made *towards* the enemy, one at 6.44 to S.E. and a second at 6.55 to S. It is regrettable that so erroneous a statement could have been made by a responsible narrator. Further, it discloses a profound ignorance of one of the leading features of the battle.

It was now that the crossing of the German T by our Battle Fleet woke Admiral Scheer out of a fool's paradise ; here was the British Fleet right across his path. He turned and fled towards the English coast. Admiral Jellicoe, unaware of his turn away, and thinking that his disappearance w⌐s momentary and due to the mist, and that he would shortly come again into sight, circled his fleet gradually round, expecting every minute to sight him again.

At 7.10, while trying to cut across the stern of

our fleet, Admiral Scheer found himself again with the British Fleet across his T. This was brought about by Jellicoe's gradual circling round while feeling for his enemy.

After describing this attempt on the part of Admiral Scheer to pass astern of the Grand Fleet at about 7.0, and finding the Grand Fleet right across his path, Mr. Churchill states, on page 152, rather disparagingly :

' Jellicoe's fleet was no doubt somewhat inconveniently arranged. He was steaming south with his divisions in echelon. In fact he now, at 7.12 p.m., was in the very position he had so disliked before his original deployment.'

Here the innocence of the amateur again peeps out. Since the leaders of the divisions were on their proper bearing to reform into line ahead, the disposition in echelon did not matter, and was no inconvenience at all. The fact that the bearing of the leaders of his divisions from each other was not at right angles to the bearing of the enemy, was what Admiral Jellicoe " disliked " " before his original deployment." He continues :

' But nevertheless in practice no serious difficulty arose.'

Of course no difficulty arose. There was absolutely no reason why one should have arisen. The point is of little interest, except to the professional tactician, but it is well to correct the disparaging impression conveyed by Mr. Churchill's remark.

On page 153 Mr. Churchill ends his description

of the short, sharp encounter between the two
fleets as follows :

1. 'Here at any rate was a moment when, as a
   glance at the map will show, it would have
   been quite easy to divide the British Fleet
   with the 5th Battle Squadron leading the
   starboard division and so take the enemy
   between two fires.'
2. 'But the British Commander-in-Chief was
   absorbed in avoiding torpedo attack by turning
   away. The range opened, the fleets separated,
   and Scheer vanished again from Jellicoe's
   view—this time for ever.'

The mistakes made by Mr. Churchill in his
tactical suggestions perhaps come largely from
glancing at a map. Considerable *study* of a map is,
as a rule, necessary before a considered opinion
can be given on any tactical point.

It is evident that at least two fast squadrons are
necessary to envelope an enemy's fleet, one to
steam up on his starboard side and one on his port
side. Only one squadron of only three ships, in
the case in point, viz. the 5th Battle Squadron,
was available. Now the information that anyone
will gather from a careful study of diagrams 11, 12,
13 is that, although the three ships of the 5th Battle
Squadron could have drawn ahead and engaged
the German Dreadnoughts on their starboard
quarter, we had no ships fast enough to support
them, or to get within range of the enemy on his
port quarter. This is clearly shown to be the case
in diagrams 11 to 13. Diagram 11 shows the 7.20

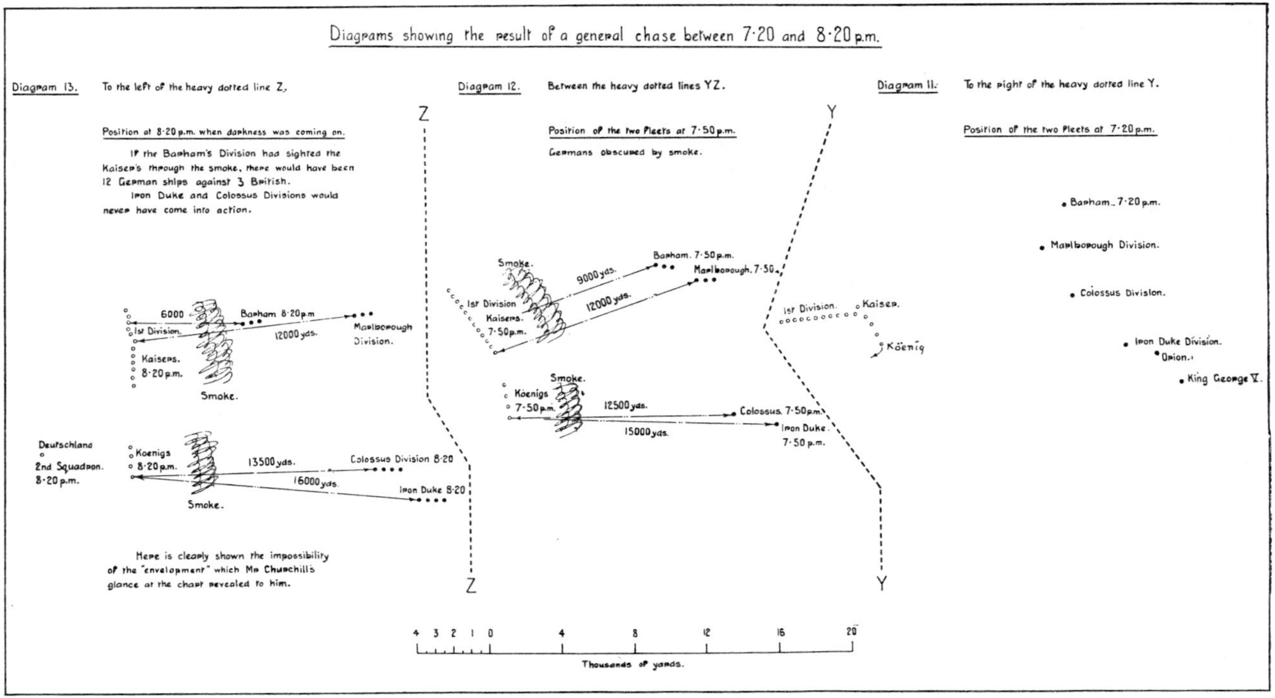

Diagrams showing the result of a general chase between 7.20 and 8.20 p.m.

Diagram 13. To the left of the heavy dotted line Z.

Position at 8.20 p.m. when darkness was coming on.

If the Barham's Division had sighted the Kaiser's through the smoke, there would have been 12 German ships against 3 British.

Iron Duke and Colossus Divisions would never have come into action.

Barham 8.20 p.m.
12000 yds.
Marlborough Division.
6000
1st Division
Kaisers. 8.20 p.m.
Smoke.

Deutschland
2nd Squadron
8.20 p.m.
Koenigs
8.20 p.m.
13500 yds.
16000 yds.
Colossus Division 8.20
Iron Duke 8.20
Smoke.

Here is clearly shown the impossibility of the "envelopment" which Mr Churchill's glance at the chart revealed to him.

Diagram 12. Between the heavy dotted lines YZ.

Position of the two Fleets at 7.50 p.m.

Germans obscured by smoke.

Smoke.
9000 yds.
Barham. 7.50 p.m.
Marlborough 7.50 p.m.
12000 yds.
1st Division
Kaisers.
7.50 p.m.

Smoke.
Koenigs
7.50 p.m.
12500 yds.
Colossus 7.50 p.m.
15000 yds.
Iron Duke
7.50 p.m.

1st Division Kaiser.
König 1q

Diagram 11. To the right of the heavy dotted line Y.

Position of the two Fleets at 7.20 p.m.

• Barham. 7.20 p.m.

• Marlborough Division.

• Colossus Division.

• Iron Duke Division.
• Orion.
• King George V.

N   Z   Y

Thousands of yards.

20   16   12   8   4   0

4 3 2 1 0

To face page 166

p.m. position of the leading divisions of the two fleets. Diagram 13 shows what would have been their position at 8.20 p.m after one hour's hard steaming. Diagram 12 shows what would have been their position at 7.50 p.m. There can be no doubt about these positions, provided that our fleet was not forced further astern than shown owing to a torpedo attack launched by the Germans.[1]

What Mr. Churchill and the majority of the critics have overlooked is that the fast *Königs* (which were faster than any of our Dreadnoughts except the 5th Battle Squadron) were leading the German advance at 7.12 p.m. and therefore were nearer our battleships than were the slower German Dreadnoughts, whose steaming speed was approximately equal to that of our battleships. The whole German Fleet was turned the moment the *Königs* sighted our battleships. The result was that, since the whole fleet was turned at the same moment *together* away from our fleet, their fastest ships were in the rear of the retreat and could easily walk away from our *Dreadnoughts*. Whereas the slower German *Dreadnoughts*, which were out of range, could, generally speaking, maintain their distance from our fleet. The older *Deutschlands* were still further away from our fleet, in fact so far off that they could not possibly be overhauled even by the 5th Battle Squadron before dark.

[1] There can be no ambiguity as regards the plotting of these diagrams, as Admiral Scheer would have had no alternative but to run away as soon as he found our fleet was following him. Every advantage lies with the fleet which is being chased during a stern chase. Moreover, though steering a safe course away from our fleet, they would at 8.40 p.m. have been only 5 miles further from the Horn Reef than they actually were at that time.

Mr. Churchill's tactics would inevitably have led to the three ships of the 5th Battle Squadron being exposed, unsupported, to the murderous fire of six German Dreadnoughts.

If, therefore, a general ' chase ' had been ordered no useful purpose would have been attained before night set in, but the Grand Fleet would then have been at dark a disorganised armada in a condition when safe night cruising would have been impossible.

There were many other points that were not brought home to Mr. Churchill in his library, but which were most important to Admiral Jellicoe on the bridge of the *Iron Duke*. To commence with, it was possible to obtain only a very vague view of the German Fleet as it emerged from the mist. The visibility was becoming less and less owing chiefly to the smoke from the guns and funnels, and the North Sea mist, making it hard to count the number of the German ships or their formation. They could only be glimpsed in the intervals between the opaque patches of smoke poured out from our own guns, and then they appeared shrouded in funnel smoke and the smoke of the guns of their own consorts. Next the German destroyers were ordered to advance and make a smoke screen, and it was behind this screen that the German Fleet turned and ran away.

Let us put ourselves in Admiral Jellicoe's place. The first glimpse of the enemy showed that the ships were steaming almost straight towards the *Iron Duke*. Splendid ! If they continued on that course they would have the head of their line smashed to atoms. Then the leading ships were seen to have turned parallel to our lines: again excellent! A broadside action with our fleet closing rapidly was the best thing that could happen so far as we were concerned. Then the next thing that happened was that the ships were lost sight of behind a screen of smoke. What did this mean ? Admiral Jellicoe knew perfectly well that it heralded a massed attack with torpedoes from the destroyer flotillas. The very manœuvre that he had been warned that the Germans intended to carry out. A deadly scheme, the intention of which was to incapacitate a number of our battleships and then to fight a battle fleet action with approximately equal numbers on each side. All the necessary factors were present, thick weather, failing light, and a broadside action heralded by a massed attack by destroyers shrouded by a smoke screen.

The problem Admiral Jellicoe had to solve appeared to him in a very different light, when viewed by him through the smoke and haze of that fast darkening evening, from what it seemed to Mr. Churchill as he threw a glance at his post-war chart with the British Fleet set out in black and the German forces printed in red, all beautifully lit up either by broad daylight or strong electric lamps. The essential difficulties of the moment that faced Admiral Jellicoe were (1) the complete blotting out of the German Fleet by smoke and his consequent inability to observe their alteration of course; and (2) the immediate danger which threatened his battleships from a torpedo attack.

Before following Mr. Churchill on these matters we must say a few words about torpedoes generally.

The torpedo was a weapon whose range had increased from eight hundred yards in 1900 to fifteen thousand yards in 1916. When the character of a weapon changes so completely in so short a time it is difficult year by year to reassess its exact functions in the various phases of naval tactics. There is, however, one outstanding fact, namely that this increase in range was of no advantage so far as night work was concerned. Darkness annihilates the value of increased range in any weapon. In daytime, however, the increase in range had been the cause of yearly pushing daylight gun-actions to the very limit at which practical hitting could be ensured. It acted like an invisible hand constantly pushing contending battle fleets more and more apart and increasing the range at which they would have to fight. It also introduced a new element into battle fighting, since independent vessels carrying torpedoes came to be attached to the fleets which could rush at high speed to a point of vantage and fire a salvo of torpedoes at the broadsides of the enemy.

Now what were the chances of such a torpedo attack succeeding? Sober calculation had shown and still shows, that two out of every five torpedoes fired on the beam of a Battle Fleet should hit ships. Since the war many trials have been carried out by firing torpedoes, without explosive charges, at a line of ships. The results, that are well known to all interested, have shown conclusively that it is futile to trust to ships individually trying to avoid the torpedoes by attempting to steer clear of the track left by them as they run through the water.

The actual figures cannot be quoted since they, rightly, are looked on as confidential, but there can be no harm in stating, what must now be common knowledge, that the inference culled from these trials leads to the belief that the chances were that at least seven of the Grand Fleet battleships would, in all probability, have been put out of action if Admiral Jellicoe had not turned his fleet away from the attack, further, that he would have incurred a very grave risk had he turned his ships *towards* the direction of attack.

The latest information at Admiral Jellicoe's disposal showed that he might have to deal with eighty-eight German destroyers in a fleet action. That is, *taking a very extreme case,* four waves of attack of sixty-six torpedoes each.

Is there any sane unbiassed person living who, had he been in Admiral Jellicoe's place, would have said ' I don't care a farthing for the threat of a torpedo attack, I will throw all caution to the winds and act as if torpedoes do not exist.' I venture to say that no responsible person would have followed such a course in war, however much they may bluster and criticise in peace time.

Before this short digression we left Admiral Jellicoe on the bridge of the *Iron Duke* faced by the menace of torpedo attack, he quite properly turned his fleet four points ' away' and saved probably some six or seven ships being sunk. Mr. Churchill, however, does not hesitate to pooh-pooh the risks. On page 113, after quoting some views expressed by Admiral Custance, he says :

'Again and again I have heard him contend that the torpedo would play only a very unimportant part in a great sea battle, and that the issue would be decided by a combination of gunfire and manœuvre. The results of Jutland seem to vindicate this unfashionable opinion.'

Here Mr. Churchill hardly gives fair prominence to the fact that the reason why the torpedo was ineffective in the Battle Fleet action was because it was defeated by Admiral Jellicoe's unpopular tactic of turning away from the attack. The main advocates of the torpedo have always recognised that it was not 'a deciding factor' in determining a fleet battle, but have insisted that it imposed certain limitations on the free action of the opposing fleet. In the case in point the massed attack caused Admiral Jellicoe to turn his ships away, and so relieved the immediate pressure on the German battleships. Exactly the class of compulsion that had been foreseen.

Most of the critics who have had the temerity to criticise the action of the Commander-in-Chief of the Grand Fleet have advocated that at this juncture he should have said metaphorically, ' I don't care a fig for torpedoes, I'll go straight for the German Fleet.' Not so Mr. Churchill, who, still not caring the fig for torpedoes, proposes an eccentric solution of the difficulty, namely that of dividing the fleet into two portions with a view to enveloping the enemy. This he advocates in spite of the fact that only one part, and that of only three ships, was fast enough to do so efficiently, and the remainder of the fleet could not get into the desired position in time to be of any value. Further, that for the last half-hour before dark the three ships of the 5th Battle Squadron would have been left unsupported while fighting six or more German Dreadnoughts.

It is now necessary to point out a gross misstatement that is made on page 153 which again is paragraphed for simplicity of analysis :

'(1) Between 6.00 and 7.30 the German flotillas had delivered no fewer than seven attacks upon the British Battle Fleet. (2) The true answer to these attacks was the counter-attack of the British flotillas and light cruiser squadrons, of which latter two were available and close at hand. These should have been ordered to advance and break up the enemy's torpedo craft, as they were fully capable of doing. Instead of using this aggressive parry Jellicoe turned his battleships away on each occasion and contact with the enemy ceased.'

Why, we wonder, does Mr. Churchill chose the times 6.00 till 7.30 ? The two Battle Fleets were not in contact till 6.25. Moreover, no general attack was made by the enemy's destroyers until 7.10 p.m.. Although one or two torpedoes were sighted by the ships of the 1st Battle Squadron earlier, one of which struck the *Marlborough.*

Three separate attacks were delivered between 7.10 and 7.30, and a fourth attack by the German 3rd and 5th flotillas was commenced ; they, however, sighted only our 11th flotilla as the battleships had turned away, so they retired without firing their torpedoes.

These inaccuracies are of little moment, however, compared with what his statement conveys (but which it is barely conceivable that it was intended to convey), namely that *seven* different attacks were made between 6.00 and 7.30 p.m. and that Admiral Jellicoe turned away *seven* times.

As a matter of fact Admiral Jellicoe turned away once, and once only, this turn taking place at 7.22 p.m., and by so doing he probably saved seven of our battleships.

Since Mr. Churchill has no experience of fleet work he may be forgiven many of the errors of which he has been guilty, but so careless a statement as the one that we have just quoted, and one so apt to mislead the general reader, is inexcusable on the part of a serious historian.

As regards (2) the 4th Light Cruiser Squadron *was* ordered to attack and break up the attempt of the enemy's destroyers; in doing this it was accompanied by the 11th Destroyer Flotilla. But it it not so easy in real warfare to break up an attack, made by brave and desperate men, as compass measurements on a chart might lead Mr. Churchill to suppose. The forces mentioned *checked* the attack, but they were powerless to prevent the enemy's destroyers firing their torpedoes within range of the Battle Fleet.

It may also be remarked that the Grand Fleet Battle Orders had assigned the very duty to the Light Cruiser Squadrons that Mr. Churchill has suggested. The order as regards destroyers is worth quoting as an example of the decentralised control that existed in the Grand Fleet :

' Take up the best position that you can for offensive action for operating against both the German Battle Fleet and its destroyers, having always in view the relative number of destroyers present on both sides.'

Other orders laid down that the light cruisers and destroyers were to adopt a vigorous offensive against enemy vessels of similar class as the first defence against torpedo attack on the Battle Fleet.

Another mistake, most misleading to the casual reader, will be found on the chart showing ' Admiral Scheer's second turn away.' Here we find entered the remark :

' Three boats of 3rd Flotilla 7.15 fired three torpedoes.'

No mention is made of the other thirty that were fired although the 7.20 positions of ships and destroyers are shown. The inevitable inference to be drawn from this careless charting is that Admiral Jellicoe turned away from an attack of three torpedoes only.

We now pass to the last paragraph on page 153.

' Beatty, however, still sought to renew the action.'

This is an innuendo that Admiral Jellicoe did not wish to renew the action. A distinct, untrue, and unworthy suggestion. Innuendoes remind one of the buttons placed in the collection plate in church, spurious in value, deceptive in purpose, and easy to disown.

We have now to follow Mr. Churchill very closely in a remarkable attempt to show that Admiral Jellicoe deserted Admiral Beatty and left him to engage the enemy unsupported. We will quote the essential portions of this covert accusation :

'At 7.45 he (*Admiral Beatty*) signalled the bearing of the enemy through the leading battleship, and at 7.47 sent the much-discussed message to the Commander-in-Chief : " Submit that the van of the battleships follow me ; we can then cut off the enemy's fleet." Almost immediately thereafter he altered course to close the enemy.'

The first thing to note is that the enemy were already cut off from the only place that they could be cut off from, namely their home ports. The signal therefore only showed that Admiral Beatty had mistaken the strategical as distinct from the tactical situation. It is a pity Mr. Churchill did not lift his eye from the tactical diagram to glance at the strategic map of the North Sea with the positions of the two fleets marked on it.

In order to explain clearly what the signal Mr. Churchill has quoted conveyed to Admiral Jellicoe, and the difficulty in which it placed him, it is necessary to cite the five signals made between 7.30 and 8.00 p.m. :

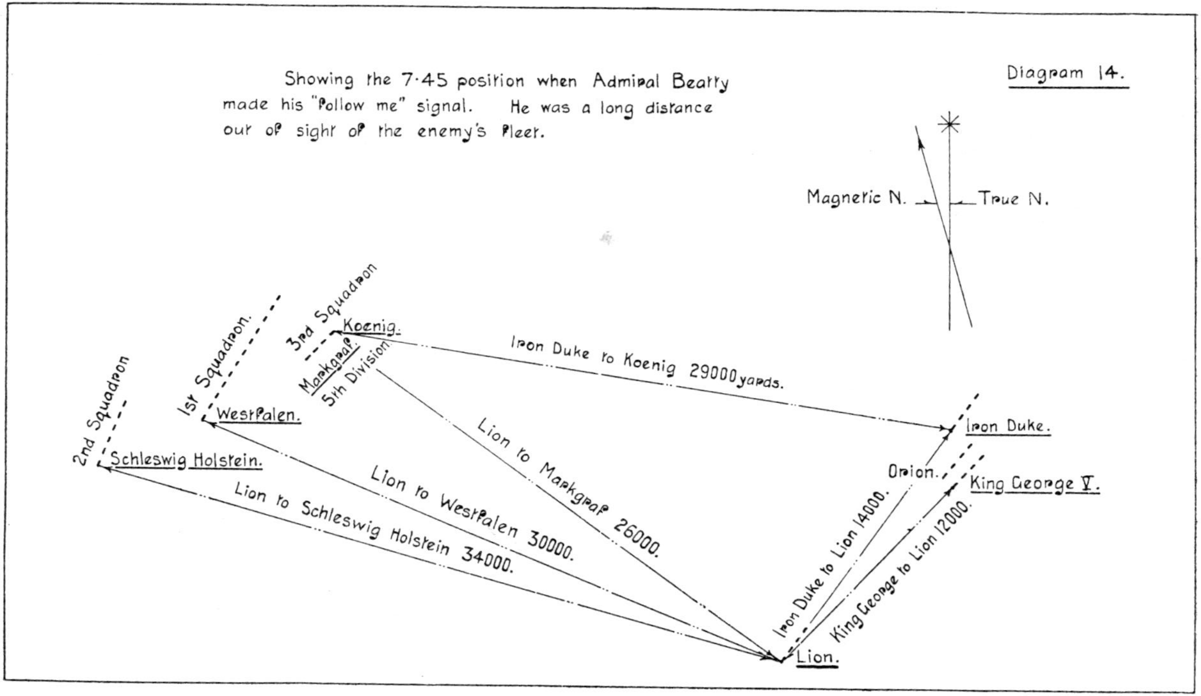
Diagram 14.
Showing the 7·45 position when Admiral Beatty made his "follow me" signal. He was a long distance out of sight of the enemy's fleet.
Magnetic N.
True N.
3rd Squadron
Koenig.
Markgraf.
5th Division
1st Squadron.
Westfalen.
2nd Squadron
Schleswig Holstein.
Iron Duke to Koenig 29000 yards.
Lion to Markgraf 26000.
Lion to Westfalen 30000.
Lion to Schleswig Holstein 34000.
Iron Duke.
Orion.
King George V.
Iron Duke to Lion 14000.
King George to Lion 12000.
Lion.

To face page 176

Time of origin.	Time of despatch.	From	Import.
(1) 7.30	7.40	*Lion* to C.-in-C. by W/T	Enemy bears from me N.W. by W. 10 to 11 miles. My position lat. 56·56 N. long., 6·16 E. Course S.W. 18 knots.

(2) This was made before the receipt of the above.

7.40	7.43	C.-in-C. to *Lion* by W/T	Present course of fleet S.W.

(3) 7.45	7.45	*Lion* to S.O. 2nd Cruiser Squadron by searchlight	Pass to leading battleship. Leading enemy battleship bears N.W. by W. Course about S.W.

The above was received in *Iron Duke* at 7.59 p.m.

(4) The signal quoted by Mr. Churchill.

7.50	7.47	*Lion* to C.-in-C. by W/T	Urgent. Submit van of battleships follows battle cruisers. We can then cut off the whole of enemy's battle fleet.

This signal was received in *Iron Duke* at 7.54 and had to be decyphered, so was not handed in to Admiral Jellicoe till shortly after 8.00 p.m., after he had ordered the alteration of course of the Battle Fleet to W. by the following signal :—

(5) 8.00	8.00	C.-in-C. General flags and W/T	Divisions separately alter course in succession to W., preserving their formation. Speed 17 knots.

Comparing these signals with one another two points at once become clear regarding the information of which Admiral Jellicoe was in possession when the signal from Admiral Beatty quoted by Mr. Churchill was handed to him.

(a) The course of the *Lion* as last signalled by Admiral Beatty was south-west. Admiral Jellicoe had just altered the course of the Battle Fleet to west. He was therefore steering with the Battle Fleet four points more *towards* the enemy than was the *Lion* by her last signal.

The battle cruisers did not alter from their south-west course until 8.10 p.m., and then only steered two points *less* towards the enemy than the Battle Fleet was steering. This point, which is one of great importance, is not mentioned by Mr. Churchill.

    (*b*) The signal (1) as worded was incorrect as the *Lion* was thirteen and a half miles from any German battleship and eighteen and a half miles from the leading one.

In these circumstances it is not to be wondered at that Admiral Jellicoe should have taken a minute or two to consider what the signal was intended to convey, for, first of all, message No. 3 put the position of the German Battle Fleet different to that in which Admiral Jellicoe knew it to be.

Secondly, the No. 4 signal, made seven minutes later, contained a proposal to cut that fleet off, when it already had been cut off from the only place from which it could have been cut off. Lastly, as it did not include the course of the *Lion* the presumption (a correct one) was that she was steering the same course as that given in her last signal, which was four points further from the enemy than the Battle Fleet was steering ! ! !

After a few minutes' consideration Admiral Jellicoe ordered the leading division of battleships to follow Admiral Beatty, but as the *Lion* was out of sight to the south-westward that division was unable to comply with the order before darkness set in.

As a matter of fact the British Battle Fleet were closing the German Battle Fleet more rapidly than were the battle cruisers so that had Admiral Jellicoe complied with Admiral Beatty's request to follow the battle cruisers the battleships would have had to draw away from the enemy.

Now to finish the quotation of Mr. Churchill's summary:

'A quarter of an hour was allowed to elapse after Jellicoe received Beatty's signal before he sent the necessary order, and in no urgent terms, to the Second Battle Squadron.'

As a matter of fact the signal was received in *Iron Duke* at 7.54 p.m., so Admiral Jellicoe would have seen it shortly after 8.00 p.m. He had just signalled to Admiral Beatty that the course of the Battle Fleet was west, and about 8.05 he told the *King George V* to follow Admiral Beatty. This time is fixed by being logged in the log of *King George V* as received at 8.07 p.m. It appears therefore that the quarter of an hour that Mr. Churchill alleges that Admiral Jellicoe took to make up his mind was nearer to five minutes, not a very long while considering the complexity of the data before him.

We will now pass to Mr. Churchill's description of the night of May 31. His commencement is most telling. The difficulties met with in night fighting and the disabilities imposed on the various arms are well and tersely put; but unfortunately soon, for want of sea-going experience, he is unable to interpret markings on his chart. We find on page 156:

'They (*the British and German minefields*) were marked as clearly as rocks or shoals, and could be avoided with almost equal certainty.'

Mr. Churchill forgets that shoals and rocks are charted by careful observation in daytime; the British mine-fields were laid always at night, mostly by mine-layers, and a few by destroyer leaders after steaming some two hundred and fifty miles. The mines might easily therefore have been any distance from five to ten miles different to their charted position. In case of uncertain charting the maximum possible error in position has to be allowed for when navigating a fleet.

In discussing the possible routes that the German Fleet might have taken to make their way home we find :

' Retreat into the Baltic by the Kattegat gave Scheer no security against being brought to battle in daylight. It involved a voyage of nearly three hundred and fifty miles, giving the faster British a long day to chase in the open sea. Jellicoe could have provided for this route by the simple process (which he did not, however, adopt) of sending a few light cruisers to watch the area and thus ensure timely information at dawn.'

We are beginning to be cautious when we read of *simple* and *easy* courses which have been discovered by Mr. Churchill and which the Commander-in-Chief of the Grand Fleet did not adopt. This particular *simple* process would have been a futile one. Had Admiral Scheer attempted the Kattegat route he would, steaming at sixteen knots, have been about one hundered and fifty miles from the Grand Fleet at dawn. It certainly would have required a long day for the Grand Fleet to have overtaken him in daylight, longer even than the one when ' the sun stood still upon Gideon and the moon in the valley of Ajalon.' Joshua only required twenty-four hours for his battle, Mr. Churchill, graspingly, demands some thirty-eight hours of daylight on the 1st of June.

Another point that Mr. Churchill has missed is that the Official History states that Admiral Jellicoe was sent the *general direction* of the routes. This is a very different thing to the full information entered on the post-war charts which were at Mr. Churchill's disposal.

Mr. Churchill dismisses the probability that Admiral Scheer would use the Ems route,

' which was long and round about, might also be dismissed as improbable.'

Doubtless this may be dismissed now that we know that the German Fleet did not make use of it ; but at 9.00 p.m. on May 31, 1916, Admiral Jellicoe would have been ill-advised to have disposed so easily of the possibility of its use by Admiral Scheer.

The distance to the Ems Channel was one hundred and eighty miles : half of this could have been covered in the dark, leaving only a little less than six hours' daylight steaming to be done. If, as Mr. Churchill suggests that he should have done, Admiral Jellicoe had steered for a point ten miles to the south-westward of the Horn Reef, the Ems passage would have been uncovered. This he calls a good movement. In view of present knowledge this may be true, but, viewed in the light of the facts before Admiral Jellicoe, this was not the case.

What were the facts as they appeared to the Admiral ?

Take, first of all, the sound of gun-firing when the 4th German Scouting Group came into contact with the British 2nd Light Cruiser Squadron. Mr. Churchill remarks :

' Firing in this quarter, though it was no proof, at least suggested that the enemy was seeking to pass astern of the British Fleet on the way to the Horn Reef. (2) But confirmation of a decisive character was at hand.'

The firing heard was that of light calibre guns. Why should Admiral Jellicoe, or Admiral Beatty, who was well able to locate approximately the direction of the firing, come to any other conclusion than the one that they did arrive at, which incidentally was the correct one, that our light cruisers and destroyers were engaging some of the lighter German vessels ? The fact of two light squadrons engaging at night was no evidence that the German battleships were crossing the stern of our fleet. That the German light cruisers were likely to be at some distance from their battleships was so probable as to be almost a certainty. That our destroyers should have come into contact with a German light cruiser division and its destroyers, which were groping in the dark looking for our battleships with a view to making a torpedo attack, was a far more probable assumption than that the German light cruisers were close ahead of their

Battle Fleet. None of the other ships of our Battle Fleet which were nearer to the firing drew the inference that the German Battle Fleet was crossing behind our fleet, or they would have reported the same to their Commander-in-Chief.

Now for (2). Mr. Churchill continues as follows :

'At 10.41 the *Iron Duke*, and at about 11.30, after it had been decoded, Sir John Jellicoe received the following electrifying message : " German Battle Fleet ordered home at 9.14 p.m. Battle cruisers in rear. Course S.S.E. ¾ E. Speed 16 knots." If this message could be trusted it meant, and could only mean, that the Germans were returning by the Horn Reef.'

Later on Mr. Churchill asks :

' But could the Admiralty message be trusted ? ' This is certainly a point to be considered.

The important signals received by Admiral Jellicoe were :

1. The Admiralty signal, time of origin 9.58 p.m., received by him at about 10.45 p.m. This message was obviously incorrect, since it placed the rear ship of the German Fleet at 9.00 p.m. eight miles to the southward of (that is approximately ahead of) the position occupied by the *King George V*, which was the leading ship of our Battle Fleet at that time. This not unnaturally tended to create a distrust of signals intercepted and decyphered by the Admiralty.

2. The second Admiralty message quoted above, which would probably have been accepted had it not been for the reports from Commodore Goodenough and the *Birmingham.*
3. The message from the Commodore at 10.15 p.m. received in *Iron Duke* at 11.38 p.m. placed the German 4th Scouting Squadron to the westward of the line of advance of the British Battle Fleet.
4. The message from the *Birmingham* at 11.30 p.m. placed the German battle cruisers thirty miles to the northward, nearly right astern of our Battle Fleet, steering a southerly course, i.e. following our fleet.

It was impossible, if the Admiralty message was correct that the German Commander-in-Chief had altered course to S.S.E. $\frac{3}{4}$ E. at 9.15 p.m., that the German battle cruisers could be astern of our fleet and steering a similar course at 11.30 p.m.

Which evidence was to be trusted by Admiral Jellicoe at 11.30 p.m., a signal intercepted by the Admiralty two hours previously, or the information signalled by one of the fleet cruisers at the moment ?

It is easy to be wise in the light of present knowledge, but at the moment matters were not at all clear. Admiral Jellicoe decided to act on the report of his own cruisers. Mr. Churchill, however, remarks :

' It is difficult to feel that this decision was not contrary to the main weight of evidence.

Certain it is that if Sir John Jellicoe had acted in accordance with the Admiralty message he would have had, even if that message had proved erroneous, a justification for his action which could never have been impugned.'

But is this so? Let us suppose that the German Fleet had made the Ems Channel and arrived safely in port. Could not Mr. Churchill have marshalled the facts against Admiral Jellicoe somewhat as follows?

> ' *Firing astern! What of that? Surely the Admiral was expecting his destroyers to be engaged, else why had he stationed them in that position? The error in the first Admiralty signal should have made him cautious in accepting a second one from the same source when the reports from two of his own ships, from ocular evidence, positively proved the enemy to be in a position which was impossible if the Admiralty signal was correct. Surely much could have happened between 9.15 p.m. and 11.30 to have caused the German Admiral to have altered his mind. If Sir John Jellicoe had acted in accordance with the evidence of his own cruisers he would have had—even if that information was incorrect—a justification for his action which could never have been impugned.'*

Unless the German Fleet had been met with and stopped, whatever action Admiral Jellicoe had taken was bound to be open to subsequent criticism.

The Admiralty at 10.10 had Admiral Scheer's message to the Airship Detachment requesting early air reconnaissance off the Horn Reef. This was never passed to Admiral Jellicoe. If it had been it might well have been the extra evidence that might have caused him to believe that Admiral Scheer would chose the Horn Reef route. Why this was never passed has never been made public. Let us hope that the Admiralty will in the near future explain this matter.

One further remark. The evidence which was before Admiral Jellicoe was also in the possession of Admiral Beatty, who likewise believed in the Ems route, as is shown by the following signal made at 4.4 a.m. on June 1 to Admiral Jellicoe when the latter ordered the fleet to turn for the Horn Reef:

'When last seen enemy was to the westward steering south-west and proceeding slowly. Zeppelin has passed astern of me steering west. Submit I may sweep south-west to locate enemy.'

If both Admiral Jellicoe and Admiral Beatty interpreted, at the time, the signals and happenings of the night in the same way, we are inclined to believe that Mr. Churchill's opinion must be somewhat tinged by knowledge that came only after the event.

Here we leave that portion of *The World Crisis* that claims to be a record of the Battle of Jutland, which, though plausible to the casual reader, is absolutely unreliable both because of the inaccuracy of many of the statements regarding the details of that fight and also because of the deductions that Mr. Churchill has drawn from them.

It must be a matter of general regret that the book unjustly impugns the professional conduct both of the Rear-Admiral commanding the 5th Battle Squadron and also that of the Commander-in-Chief of the Grand Fleet.

INDEX

A

191